THE DRESSMAKER'S HANDBOOK
COUTURE
OF
SEWING TECHNIQUES

ESSENTIAL STEP-BY-STEP TECHNIQUES FOR PROFESSIONAL RESULTS

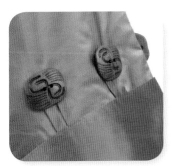 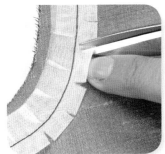  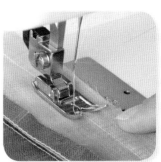

LYNDA MAYNARD

A QUARTO BOOK
Published in 2010 by
A&C Black Publishers
36 Soho Square
London W1D 3QY
www.acblack.com

ISBN 978-1-408-12759-9

A CIP record for this book is available from
the British Library.

Conceived, designed and produced by
Quarto Publishing plc
The Old Brewery
6 Blundell Street
London N7 9BH

QUAR.COU

Senior Editor: Lindsay Kaubi
Art Editor and Designer: Elizabeth Healey
Art Director: Caroline Guest
Copy Editors: Carol Spier and Liz Dalby
Photographers: Simon Pask and
Martin Norris
Picture Researcher: Sarah Bell
Creative Director: Moira Clinch
Publisher: Paul Carslake

Colour separation by PICA digital Pte Ltd
in Singapore
Printed in China by Toppan Leefung
Printing Ltd

10 9 8 7 6 5 4 3 2 1

THE DRESSMAKER'S HANDBOOK

COUTURE

OF

SEWING TECHNIQUES

Contents

INTRODUCTION

*M*y interest in sewing began in early childhood at the age of seven. I was inspired by my mother's pastel-coloured pillow slips. One day while she was away at work, I took one and created my first dress by simply cutting a circular opening for my head and one for each arm. I proudly wore my first 'shift' around the neighbourhood and the excitement grew. I next helped myself to two more pillow slips and engineered a tiered concoction. The next venture was a real dress made with purchased yardage. I had the good sense to fold the yardage so as to have two layers. I positioned myself on the fabric and directed my best friend to draw around my body with a crayon. Wherever she encountered an obstacle (arms and head) the indication was to create an opening. My brilliance ended there, however. Fabric is two-dimensional, while the human body has a third dimension. I was a skinny child, which is the only way this dress had a chance. I also lacked the good sense to add seam allowances. Because there was no machine available, I stitched the dress together by hand. I proudly put the dress on. It was impossible to walk, but that didn't matter, I could hop. Upon discovering her missing pillow slips and my sad attempt at dressmaking, my wise mother sought out private sewing lessons for me and the rest is history.

My particular focus when sewing a garment has always been technique and detail. This is what elevates a garment to the status of couture. One must begin with good quality fabric, and then come the details. The extra painstaking steps are cumulative and serve to produce a superior product. One can compare a ready-to-wear garment with a couture version of the same garment and you will know that the couture creation is better. It's in the hang, the fit, the feel and the details.

Among the details I've included in this book are the satin pocket bag, which feels soft and luxurious, the organza bubble at the hem, which prevents a dress or skirt from collecting about the knees; the couture waistband is clean and crisp, yet ultimately comfortable, and the high waist facing features boning as a hidden ally. Some of the decorative details included in the book are the twin-needle hem, a professional yet decorative finish, the ribbon-trimmed collar band, which adds allure to a simple shirt, the silk charmeuse flange with its picot stitch, adding dimension and flutter to a lightweight blouse. You will also find a thorough exploration of couture bindings, a look at designer underpinnings and a directory of luxury fabrics used in couture sewing.

My particular passion for technique has inspired me to study designer and vintage clothing for the secrets they may contain. Also, I enjoy experimenting with various methods of handling a specific construction challenge. This collecting of techniques and designer details led to this book; I hope you enjoy them as much as I do, and possibly you will be inspired to develop new ones of your own.

Lynda Maynard

COUTURE TECHNIQUE SELECTOR

Bindings and Finishes

BANDED V-NECK ON KNIT FABRIC 18
The V-neckline is a focal point of a garment and should be done well because inaccuracy is glaring. This band overlaps at the point, a feature that gracefully enhances the neckline.

BANDED V-NECK ON WOVEN FABRIC 22
This method of finishing a V-neck can be employed by beginning as well as experienced sewers. It adds no additional bulk, yet provides maximum stability.

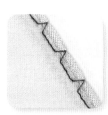

RIBBON BANDED V-NECK 24
Ribbon is a nice alternative to self-fabric for a banded finish on a V neckline. Use this technique when you want a delicate, clean-yet-stable finish for a garment made of soft, thin, firmly woven fabric.

BANDED CURVED NECKLINE 26
If you're finishing a curved neckline, this bias-band edge eliminates the need for a facing and adds definition. This finishing technique is appropriate for linens and light-to medium-weight cottons and silks and works for armholes as well as at the neck.

DOUBLE-FOLD SILK CHARMEUSE BINDING 30
This technique may be used successfully on most woven fabrics with a flat surface. For the samples, both the binding and garment fabric are silk charmeuse – however, the charmeuse binding works just as well on cottons, linens, rayons and other silks.

DOUBLE-FOLD BINDING ON CHIFFON 34
Here is a way to add a charmeuse binding to chiffon. Finishing the edges of anything made from chiffon can be a daunting task. But silk organza comes to the rescue.

FREE-FLOW CHARMEUSE BINDING ON CHIFFON 36
This is an innovative method for hemming chiffon. Double-fold silk charmeuse binding is employed to provide an artfully clean finish to the hem while adding a subtle shimmer of light and movement.

PIPED DOUBLE-FOLD BINDING ON WOVEN FABRIC 37
This is the twin-sister technique to Double-Fold Silk Charmeuse Binding on page 34. Charmeuse is so fluid, it's tricky to handle, but when your fabric is more stable, this technique will produce a similar effect with a lot less effort. This version is sewn first to the wrong side of the garment, and then wrapped to the front, with piping tucked under the edge on the right side.

Design Details: On Show

Design Details: Concealed

LINING/BINDING SKIRT PANELS 84

This technique works well on seams with minimal curves. It is suitable for panel skirts, trousers and unstructured rectangular jackets. It results in the garment being lined and seams finished with minimal effort.

COUTURE WAISTBAND 86

The couture method of constructing a waistband results in a superior product: the band does not roll, yet it is comfortable, lies flat and there is no extra bulk.

HIGH-WAIST COUTURE FACING 88

This approach to constructing a waist facing works well on any waistline where a waistband is not desired. The channel stitching and the bones add structure and support while maintaining a clean line.

EASY TWIN-NEEDLE HEM 90

This hem gives your garment a sporty, energetic look – with no rippling. It is especially good for knit or woven fabrics with Lycra introduced to provide some stretch.

ORGANZA 'BUBBLE' HEM FINISH 92

To prevent the lower edge of a sheath dress or skirt from collapsing close to the legs, slip a folded bias band of organza between the hem allowance and garment body to make a bubble-like spacer inside the hem.

FACED HEM 94

A faced hem is the perfect way to finish a skirt where a deep hem is required. Facing pieces from the skirt pattern are sewn to the lower edge and pressed to the wrong side, where they fit perfectly.

HORSEHAIR BRAID HEM 96

To support a hem and give it more rigidity, you can sew horsehair braid (or 'crin trim') to the hem. Horsehair braid supports the hem without adding bulk and keeps it from collapsing.

CONCEALING HORSEHAIR BRAID IN THE HEM 97

Horsehair braid has a rough texture that could, if not totally concealed, snag tights. For this reason it is best to ensure that it is fully concealed.

BALANCED DART 98

By balancing the dart with extra fabric, a flatter, smoother finish can be achieved, even though fabric has been added.

COUTURE DART 100

This dart technique works well on all fabrics, and it is essential when working with sheers. There are no unsightly thread ends at the tip of the dart… just a clean, graceful finish.

SATIN POCKET BAGS 102

The satin pocket bag is a luxurious detail, not meant to be seen by the casual observer but sure to enhance the mood of the wearer when the sumptuous feel of satin greets your fingers when you slip your hand into your pocket.

WAISTLINE 'FLIP-OUT' POUCH 105

A little zipped hanging pocket to add to the inside of trousers or skirts to provide secure hidden storage for a credit card, change or lipstick.

THE COUTURIER'S KIT

The wide array of machines, feet and haberdashery available for sewing is an invitation to expand your horizons. Leaping out of your comfort zone and experimenting with equipment is imperative to growth and enhancing your body of sewing knowledge. You will learn the importance of having just the right needle or foot to complete the job as you gain experience – but on the next few pages you will find a suggested 'Couturier's Kit' of items that you will find very useful when working on the techniques in this book.

SEWING MACHINE FEET

It is not required to own all of these sewing machine feet but each one certainly helps with specific tasks. Many sewers become frustrated because they are unaware of the help available with the use of the proper foot.

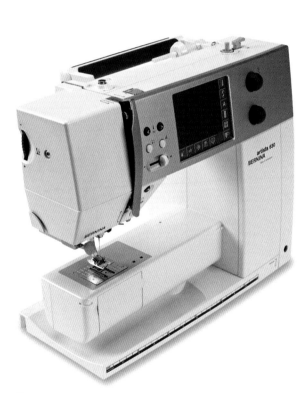

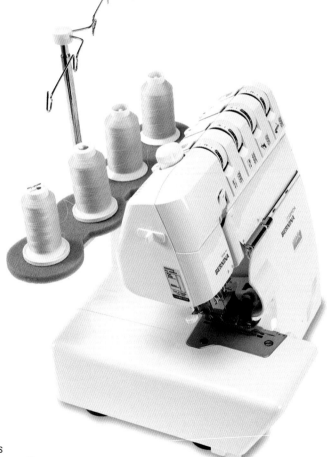

SEWING MACHINE

Sewing machines have evolved into computerized devices that are capable of highly technical manoeuvres. There are special machines designed for specific tasks. In fact, there is a machine for almost each task in the manufacturing process: machines to install sleeves, buttonhole machines, hemmers, rufflers, binders, etc. The home sewing enthusiast, however, usually assesses her skill level and her requirements, and purchases a machine to fulfil her needs. It is important to read about and try out various makes and models to find a comfortable 'fit'.

OVERLOCKER

Overlockers have come into general use and many sewers have one to accompany their basic sewing machine. They perform many functions and produce a manufactured, ready-to-wear look. As with any other major purchase, research and experiment to find the one that suits your needs.

Cording Foot: This foot has a hollow space that holds the cord securely in place while attaching it to the garment.

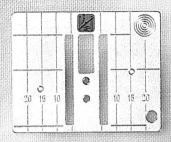

Single-Hole Throat Plate: This throat plate does not allow sideways needle movement. The opening is very small, so there is more control when working with delicate fabrics. The likelihood of the fabric being drawn into the mechanism of the machine is greatly reduced.

Roller Foot: This foot grasps the top layer of fabric so it will feed at the same rate as the bottom layer, allowing more control without added friction.

Top Stitch Foot: This foot has a built-in guide which assists with more even stitching.

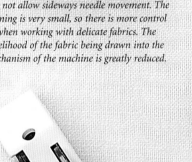

Walking Foot: For long seams, hems on stretch fabric, multiple fabric layers.

Straight Stitch Foot: For straight stitching (especially on fine fabric). Works in combination with the single-hole throat plate.

Zip Foot: When there is more bulk on one side than the other, this foot allows stitching directly next to the bulk, for example, zip teeth or a cord.

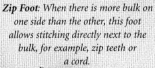

Knit Foot: This foot is shorter and the toes are slightly lifted so it does not push the fabric.

Pintuck Foot: For creating twin-needle tucks to decorate fabric.

SEWING MACHINE NEEDLES

Needles fall into a similar category as sewing machine feet. The right needle ensures success with specific fabrics. It is recommended, that you purchase the appropriate needle before beginning a new project or working with a new fabric. Also, it is of great importance to change needles regularly, since they become dull and can snag or mar your fabric.

Twin Needles

Two or three needles fixed to a single body for parallel rows of stitching.

Twin Needle For Wovens: *This needle stitches two parallel rows of stitching at the same time, producing a professional, yet decorative overall stitch.*

Twin Needle For Knits: *This needle performs the same function as above, but has a slightly rounder point to push the knit fibres aside.*

Quilting Needle:

This needle has a longer point so it can sew through multiple layers.

Sharp Universal Needle:

This needle is generally used for sewing most woven fabrics.

Microtex Needle:

This needle has a very sharp point and is appropriate for sewing silks and chiffons.

Stretch Needle:

This needle is used for fabrics containing Lycra/ Spandex. Due to its long scarf, it helps to prevent skipped stitches.

Pinking shears

SHEARS AND SCISSORS

Shears for cutting fabric are a must, but so are tailor-point shears for getting into tight corners. Pinking shears provide a great seam finish and pelican scissors assist in close trimming of fabric layers.

Dressmaker's shears (right), pelican scissors (above left), tailor-point shears (above right).

Safety pins

SHARP PINS

Absolutely indispensable in the whole process of garment construction. Pins need to be sharp to avoid snagging or marring the fabric.

Topstitching thread

Dressmaker's pins

RULERS AND CURVES

Well, these are a must! Straight rulers and skirt curves are all required for pattern work as well as garment construction. The clear plastic ones have the added benefit of transparency to help reduce errors.

Ruler and skirt curve

HAIRGRIP

This everyday item is supremely helpful in turning fabric tubes, such as spaghetti straps.

PATTERN WEIGHTS

This is a wonderful method of securing the pattern on the fabric before cutting. Pins can snag or mar the fabric and applying weights takes much less time.

TISSUE PAPER

This comes in handy as a temporary stabilizer when working with sheer, fluid fabrics such as charmeuse and chiffon. It can be placed under the fabric to facilitate cutting.

CHALK

We all need a method to mark our fabric for construction. There are several options on the market, including pencils, chalk wheels and soapstone. Find one that suits your purposes.

STEAM IRON AND IRONING BOARD

Pressing as you work is almost more important than the sewing. It is essential to press at each step of the process for maximum results. Once the garment is completed, several important areas are no longer accessible and it is too late to flatten or steam out puckers and folds. Steam helps set design and construction details.

PRESSING AIDS

Pressing aids such as a press cloth, seam stick (seam roll), point presser and point turner are inexpensive and indispensable. These provide great assistance during the pressing process and they help to produce a superior product.

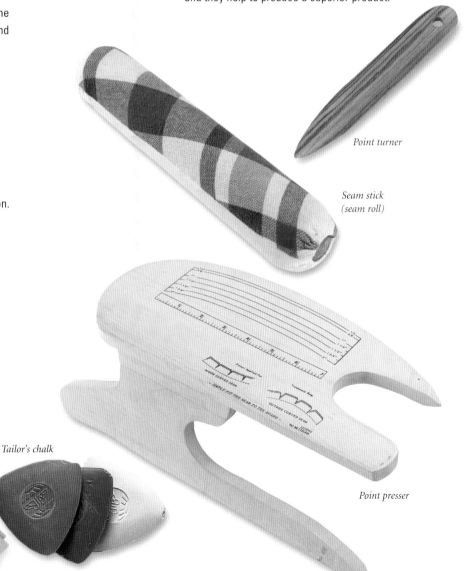

Point turner

Seam stick (seam roll)

Tissue paper and pattern weights

Tailor's chalk

Point presser

CHAPTER ONE

BINDINGS AND FINISHES

The binding techniques in this chapter have been developed to make them cleaner, easier and timesaving, resulting in professional, visually appealing garments.

Traditional facings have always been the dressmaker's nemesis. They are the pesky pattern pieces that seem to fly off the workspace never to be seen again. Also, they tend to be bulky and not lie flat against the body – facings seem to make an appearance without an invitation. They roll out of the garment and advertise brand and size to casual observers.

These techniques display ways of finishing outer edges and curves of garments that are facing-free. They are versatile and have a broad application across a number of different types and styles of garments.

Precise finish

Precision in executing edge finishes will create clean, graceful, figure-enhancing lines.

Giorgio Armani, Spring/Summer 2010, Paris Fashion Week

Banded V-Neck on Knit Fabric

The V-neckline is a focal point of a garment and should be done well because inaccuracy is glaring. This band overlaps at the point, a feature that gracefully enhances the neckline and can be successfully accomplished on various angles with equal ease. Use this technique when you want a clean, simple method to finish and highlight a V-neckline and don't want to get involved with the more complicated and tedious process of making a band that mitres at the point of the V. The fabric for the band may be the same colour as the garment or a contrast.

- Fusible interfacing for knits: this allows the knit to retain some stretch for comfort.
- Twin needle for topstitching, optional
- Foot designed to sew knits, recommended

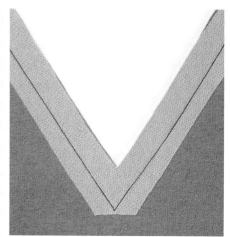

Stabilize the neckline

1. Interface the neckline

Cut a piece of fusible interfacing the shape of the neckline for each garment piece, making it the width of the seam allowance plus 1cm (⅜"). Fuse each strip to the wrong side of its piece, positioning it so it covers the seam allowance. This will stabilize the area and facilitate smoother topstitching.

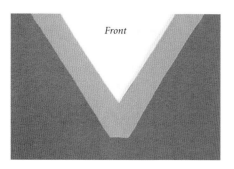

Front

Back

2. Stitch along the seamline

Staystitch the entire neckline directly on the seamline using a stitch length of 2.5mm (10 stitches per inch). Near the point of the V, shorten the stitch length to 1 or .75mm (24 stitches per inch). This tiny stitch eliminates the need for backstitching and further reinforces the point.

Note
- It is of the utmost importance to have the point of the V perfectly situated and not offset to the left or right. For this reason, it is helpful to mark the V area with a ruler and a fine chalk line before staystitching.

PREPARE THE BAND

3. Cut the neckband strip

Sew and press the shoulder seams. Measure the length of the entire neckline and add 10cm (4"); this is the length to cut the band. Decide how wide you want the band to be and add the width of your seam allowance; double this dimension to find the width to cut the band. Cut the band in your determined dimensions on the crossways grain of the knit fabric – so that the stretch runs the length of the band. This makes it easier to apply the band to the back neckline curve.

4. Fold and press the strip

Fold the neckband strip in half lengthways, right side out, and press. You may overlock the long cut edge for a professional look.

ATTACH THE BAND

5. Position and stitch in place

Place the garment right side up. Align the cut edges of the band with those of the garment, leaving a tail about 5cm (2") long extending past the point of the V as shown; pin at the V and a short way up the neckline but not around the back of the neck. Once the band has been correctly positioned, it is easier to stitch from the wrong side, where the staystitching is visible. Starting exactly at the point, stitch directly on top of the staystitching. Use a tiny stitch setting, .75 to 1mm (24 stitches per inch), near the point and don't backstitch; backstitching will cause unnecessary thread build-up and adds bulk.

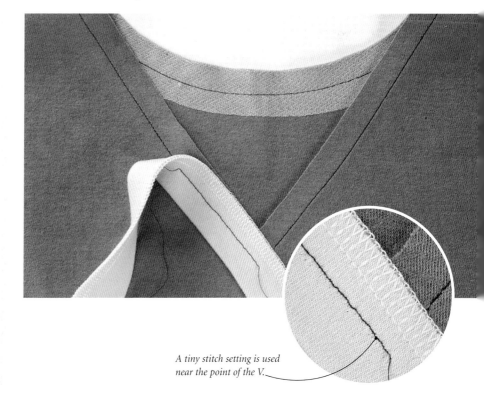

A tiny stitch setting is used near the point of the V.

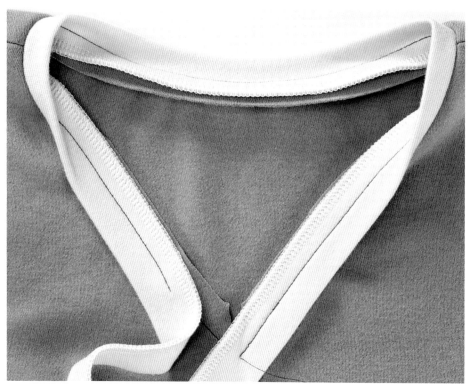

6. Continue stitching

Continue around the neck, gently coaxing the band to lie flat around the back neckline curve. Stop stitching about 2.5cm (1") before you reach the V point (or at least as far as the band width); this creates a space for the band end to overlap.

Note

- For those of you who are wondering which way the overlap will form, the side of the band stitched first will be on top.

7. Press and trim the neckline

Press the work as sewn to embed the stitches, then very carefully (using sharp scissors) clip only the garment fabric to-but-not-through the staystitching at the V. Grade the seam allowances (the allowance closest to the body should be the narrowest) and press them all towards the garment. The band will now fill in the V-neckline and the allowances will support it.

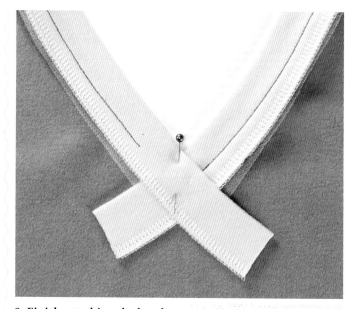

8. Finish attaching the band

With the garment wrong side up, slide the unattached end of the band over the secure end and pin it in place.

Note

- Now is the time to check and make sure your band is an even width all the way around the neckline.

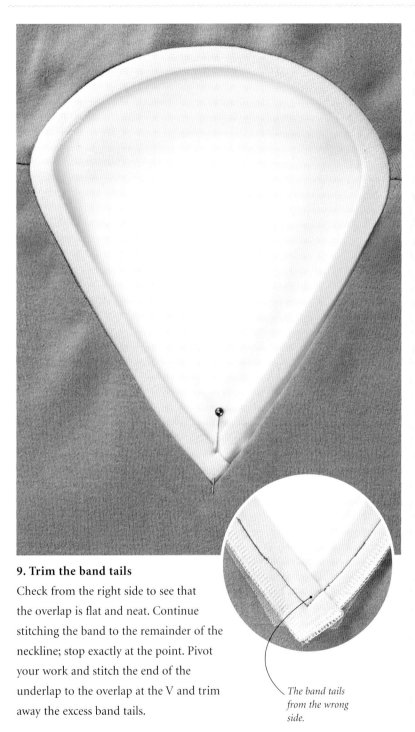

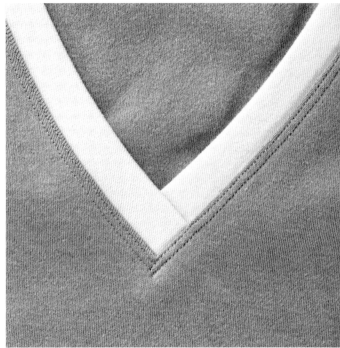

10. Topstitch the neckline

Topstitch from the right side through all thicknesses. You may use a twin needle or contrasting thread for added panache.

9. Trim the band tails

Check from the right side to see that the overlap is flat and neat. Continue stitching the band to the remainder of the neckline; stop exactly at the point. Pivot your work and stitch the end of the underlap to the overlap at the V and trim away the excess band tails.

The band tails from the wrong side.

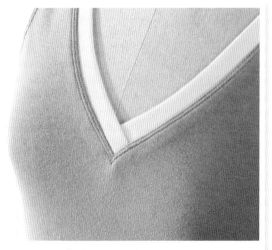

Style suggestion

- The band finish is a great way to showcase the V-neckline on this T-shirt.

BANDED V-NECK ON WOVEN FABRIC

This method of finishing a V-neck can be employed by beginning as well as experienced sewers. This is a companion technique to Banded V-Neck on Knit Fabrics, page 18, with a couple of adjustments. There is no need to interface the entire neckline because you are working with woven, non-stretch fabrics. However, it is imperative to stabilize the point of the V for successful implementation of the technique. Silk organza is a good choice for this because it is lightweight and strong. It adds no bulk, yet provides maximum stability.

- A scrap of silk organza 3.75cm (1½") square
- Twin needle for topstitching, optional

STABILIZE THE NECKLINE

1. Interface the point of the V

Hand-tack the square of silk organza to the wrong side of the garment just below the cut edge of the V. Although it's tempting to use a bit of fusible interfacing instead, a fusible is sometimes visible on the finished garment and therefore not optimal. The edges of the organza are pinked and loose and so will not imprint onto the face of the garment.

2. Stitch along the seamline

Staystitch the entire neckline directly on the seamline using a stitch length of 2.5mm (10 stitches per inch). Near the point of the V, shorten the stitch length to 1 or .75mm (24 stitches per inch). This tiny stitch eliminates the need for backstitching and further reinforces the point. Backstitching in this area can pull the garment into the netherworld beneath the throat plate and cause a mini crisis.

MAKE THE BAND

3. Cut the neckband strip

Sew the shoulder seams and press the allowances open. Because you're working with woven fabric, you'll need a bias strip of fabric for the band – this will enable it to follow the back neckline curve. Measure the length of the entire neckline and add 10cm (4"); this is the length to cut the band. To find the width, first decide how wide you want the band to be and add the width of your seam allowance; double this dimension and add a bit more to account for shrinkage when you stretch-press the band (see opposite). The amount to add varies from 3mm to 1cm (⅛" to ⅜") depending on the fabric. Cut a bias strip of the required size.

4. Press, fold and press the strip

Stretch press the bias strip (see right). Then fold the strip in half lengthways, right side out, and press again. You may overlock the long cut edge for a more professional look.

5. Attach the band

To attach the band, follow steps 5 through 8 of Banded V-Neck on Knit Fabric, pages 18–21.

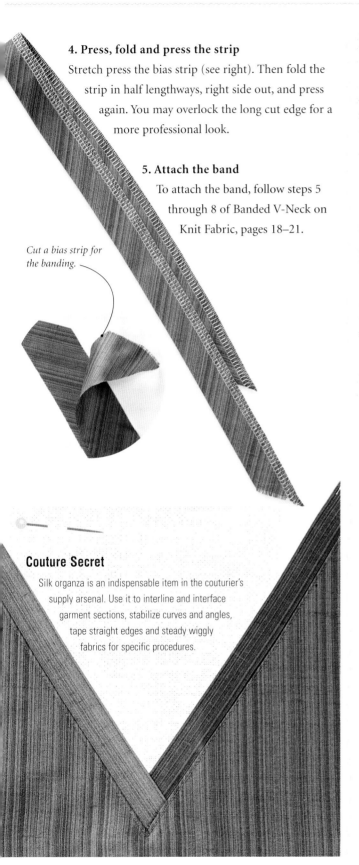

Cut a bias strip for the banding.

Couture Secret

Silk organza is an indispensable item in the couturier's supply arsenal. Use it to interline and interface garment sections, stabilize curves and angles, tape straight edges and steady wiggly fabrics for specific procedures.

Couture Secret

One of the advantages of this method of handling a V-neck on a garment made of woven fabric is that the band provides support at the point of the V. When a traditional facing is used instead of a band, the seam allowance is clipped at the V, folded down onto the body, and pressed flat on either side of the point, leaving a bit of a crater below the point that is not attractive.

Stretch-pressing

Once a bias strip has been cut out, be sure to 'stretch-press' it before sewing it to your garment. This important step prevents the strip from rippling and pulling later. Pin one end of the strip to your pressing surface and slightly pull the strip as you steam with the iron. The bias will shrink and become narrower. This is why you start with a wide strip.

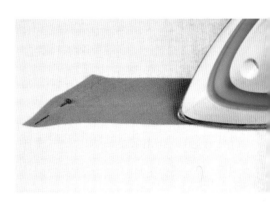

Style suggestion

• This technique works well on bateau necklines also, since each shoulder seam join functions as a V. Try using a contrasting fabric or colour, or experiment with bias stripes for added dash.

RIBBON-BANDED V-NECK

Ribbon is a nice alternative to self-fabric for a banded finish on a V-neckline. Use this technique when you want a delicate, clean-yet-stable finish for a garment made of soft, thin, firmly woven fabric such as the cotton batiste shown here. If you like, you can add a zigzag stitch embellishment to the applied ribbon to create a picot edge – this variation is charming and has a refined sensibility. This is a great neckline and armhole finish, but it may be used elsewhere as well.

SEWING TOOLS AND MATERIALS

- Soft ribbon (rayon works well), 1.25cm (1½") wide and a bit longer than the neckline circumference

- Small, sharp scissors for close trimming; stork scissors are ideal

STABILIZE THE NECKLINE
1. Stitch along the seamline

Sew the garment shoulder seams and press. Staystitch the neckline directly on the seamline using a stitch length of 2.5mm (10 stitches per inch). Near the point of the V, shorten the stitch length to 1 or .75mm (24 stitches per inch). This tiny stitch eliminates the need for backstitching and further reinforces the point.

ATTACH THE RIBBON
2. Position and stitch in place

Place the garment right side up. Beginning at the V, position the ribbon along the neckline so that about 3mm (⅛") extends into the seam allowance as shown. Follow steps 5 and 6 of Banded V-Neck on Knit Fabrics, pages 19–20, to sew on the ribbon and press it towards the neck opening.

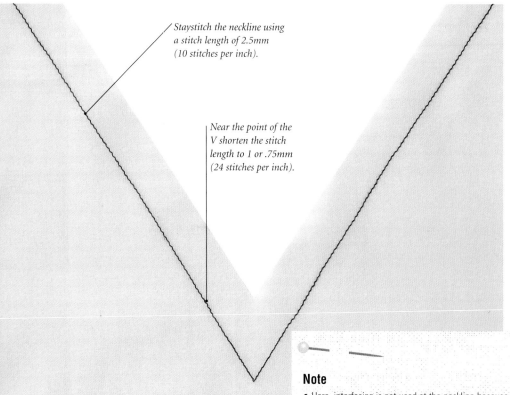

Staystitch the neckline using a stitch length of 2.5mm (10 stitches per inch).

Near the point of the V shorten the stitch length to 1 or .75mm (24 stitches per inch).

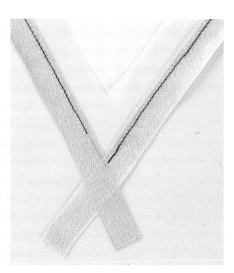

Note
- Here, interfacing is not used at the neckline because there would be show-through; however, if you feel the need for more control, use a single-hole throat plate and a straight-stitch foot when staystitching. A single layer of tissue paper placed between the fabric and the feed dogs works as a temporary stabilizer.

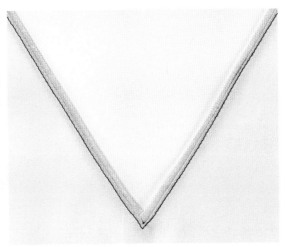

Couture Secret
You may be wondering why the garment seam allowance is not trimmed before the ribbon is applied. Leaving the wider allowance when you're applying a band, especially on curves, increases accuracy, ease of handling and stability. It's preferable to trim the seam allowances later.

3. Trim the seam allowances

Turn the garment wrong side up. Trim seam allowance on the garment neckline to a scant 3mm (⅛") – to be slightly narrower than the ribbon seam allowance; this way the ribbon will cover the raw edges when the band is finished. Take care not to nick the ribbon.

5. Overlap the ends and topstitch

Follow step 7 of Banded V-Neck on Knit Fabrics (page 20), folding and pressing the remainder of the ribbon in half as you go. Then topstitch the neckline through all thicknesses very close to edge of the garment. To set the topstitching position, place the needle directly on top of the seamline and then move the needle position one notch over.

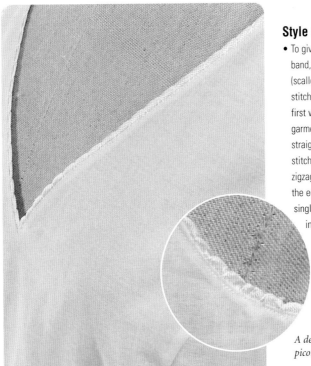

Style suggestion

- To give a softer look to a ribbon band, you could finish it with a picot (scallop) detail using the blind hem stitch. It's not necessary to topstitch first when you do this. Position your garment in your machine so that the straight portion of the blind hem stitch falls on the garment and the zigzag stitch crosses and falls off the edge of the band – it's this single zigzag that pulls the band into a scallop. Test this on a sample to see how it works.

A detail of the picot edge.

4. Fold the ribbon

On the side of the V where the ribbon is anchored all the way to the point, fold the ribbon in half lengthways to the wrong side of the garment – so it covers the stitches; press.

BANDED CURVED NECKLINE

If you're finishing a curved neckline, this bias-band edge eliminates the need for a facing and adds definition (it's a frame of sorts); it can bring a splash of vitality to a simple garment if solid and print fabrics or contrasting colours are combined. It's a clean, stable finish and it adds cachet to both sporty and dressy clothes. This finishing technique is appropriate for linens and light- to medium-weight cottons and silks and works for armholes as well as at the neck.

STABILIZE THE NECKLINE
1. Stitch along the seamline
Sew the shoulder seams and press the allowances open. Staystitch the entire neckline directly on the seamline using a stitch length setting of 2.5mm (10 stitches per inch).

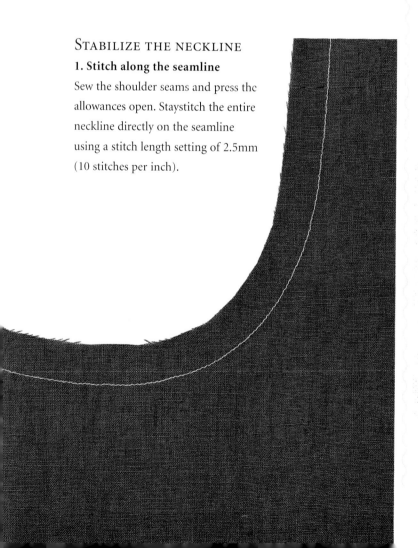

- Twin needle
- Silk organza, to use as a press cloth

PREPARE THE BAND
2. Cut the bias strip
Measure the length of the entire neckline and add 10cm (4"); this is the length to cut the strip. To find the width, double the seam allowance depth, add 2.5cm (1") and add a bit more to account for shrinkage when you stretch-press the band (see page 23). The amount to add varies, somewhere from 3mm to 1cm (⅛" to ⅜") depending on the fabric. Cut a bias strip of the required size.

Note
- Here is an example to illustrate the rather dramatic difference stretch pressing can make. Each strip began 5cm (2") wide. Notice the narrower width after the pressing. The finished width is 4.4cm (1¾"), 6mm (¼") narrower than it started. The pressed band will not be wobbly or twisty when applied, but smooth and even.

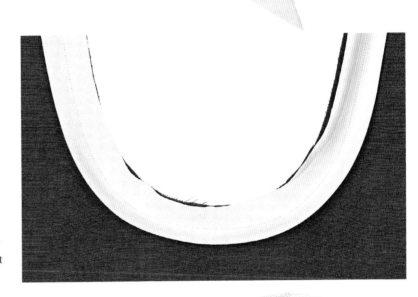

3. Press, fold and press the strip

Stretch press the bias strip (see page 23).
Press under 6mm (¼") on one end of
the strip. Then fold the strip in half
lengthways, right side out, and press again.

ATTACH THE BINDING

4. Position and stitch in place

Place the garment right side up. Position
the bias strip on top, beginning at the
centre back with the end that has been
folded under and aligning the cut edges
of the bias with the neckline edge. Begin
stitching about 2.5cm (1") from the centre
back, stitching exactly on the staystitching.
As you sew, manipulate the binding so that
it follows the curve, but do not stretch it.

5. Join the binding ends

Stop stitching about 2.5cm (1") from
the centre back. Determine where the
two ends will meet at the centre back
and join them in a seam on the straight
grain, using the pressed under edge
as a stitching guide. Trim the seam
allowances to 6mm (¼") and press
open. Finish stitching the last bit of
the binding to the garment.

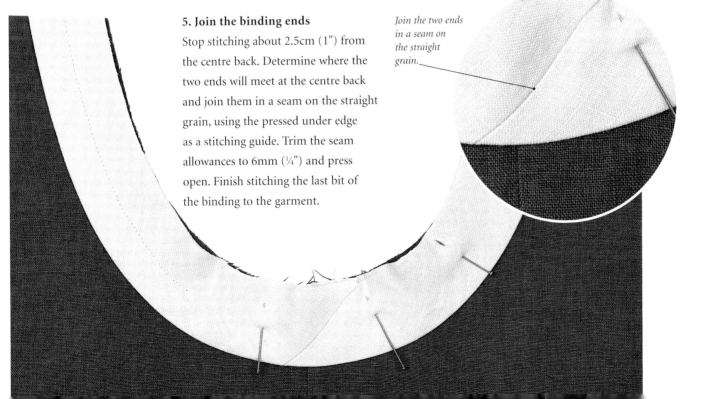

*Join the two ends
in a seam on
the straight
grain.*

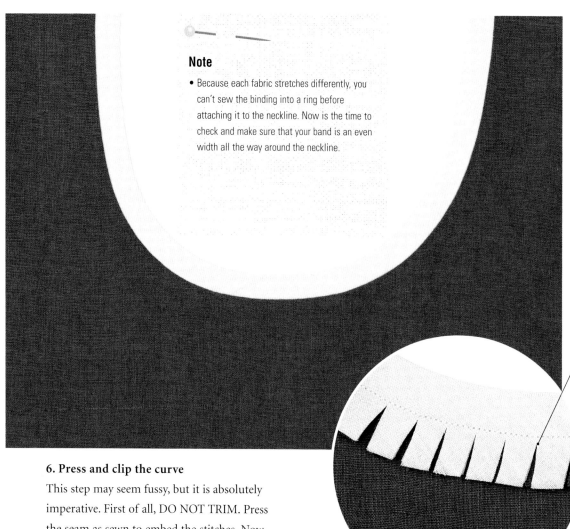

Note

- Because each fabric stretches differently, you can't sew the binding into a ring before attaching it to the neckline. Now is the time to check and make sure that your band is an even width all the way around the neckline.

Clipping allows the seam allowance to lie flat.

6. Press and clip the curve

This step may seem fussy, but it is absolutely imperative. First of all, DO NOT TRIM. Press the seam as sewn to embed the stitches. Now, clip the allowances along the entire curve through all thicknesses. The cuts will allow the seam allowance to splay and lie flat. Press the seam allowances onto the wrong side of the garment and the band towards the neckline.

Couture Secret

Silk organza functions as a great press cloth. It's transparent, so you can see if unwanted creases are forming beneath it and stop pressing to smooth out the fabric, and it also keeps your fabric from glazing, which is caused by too much steam and pressure on a fabric.

7. Overlock-finish the allowances

Overlock the seam allowance along the entire neckline, trimming it to about 6mm (¼") and being careful not to catch the garment. Keep the clips spread open so that the allowance will still lie flat against the garment.

8. Pin and topstitch the binding

With the garment right-side up, lightly press the neckline again and pin the seam allowance in place. Using a twin needle, topstitch from the right side of the garment through all thicknesses, stitching close to the band as shown.

Style suggestion

- This bias-band edging provides such a clean, well-defined approach to managing curves on simple shapes.

DOUBLE-FOLD SILK CHARMEUSE BINDING

This technique may be used successfully on most woven fabrics with a flat surface. For the samples, both the binding and garment fabric are silk charmeuse – however, the charmeuse binding works just as well on cottons, linens, rayons and other silks.

- Microtex needle or sharp needle
- Good thread, same colour as binding fabric
- Topstitch foot, recommended

STABILIZE THE NECKLINE

1. Stitch along the seamline

Staystitch the individual pieces (back and front). Sew the shoulder seams and press the allowances open. Staystitch the entire neckline directly on the seamline using a stitch length setting of 2.5mm (10 stitches per inch). This prevents the neckline from stretching during handling and acts as a visual guide for applying the binding. For easier handling, place a single layer of tissue paper between the garment and the feed dogs as a temporary stabilizer.

PREPARE THE BINDING

2. Cut the bias strip

Measure the length of the entire neckline and add 10cm (4"); this is the length to cut the strip. Decide how wide you want the finished binding to be and multiply this dimension by 6 or 7. Some width will be lost when you stretch-press the binding (see page 23), so read step 3 below and make a sample to see how wide your strip should be. Cut a bias strip of the required size.

3. Prepare the double-fold bias strip

Stretch press the bias strip (page 23). Now follow the photo sequence opposite to make the double-fold strip.

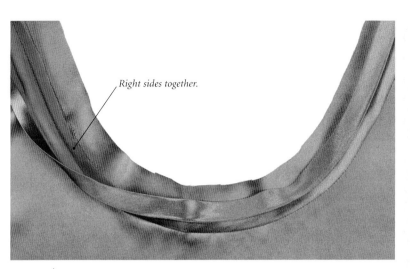

Right sides together.

ATTACH THE BINDING

4. Position and stitch in place

Place the garment right side up. Open the folded bias strip and place it right side down on the garment, with the end at the centre back neckline; position it so the strip lies on the garment side of the staystitching and the cut edge of the narrower side is aligned against the staystitching as shown. Begin stitching about 2.5cm (1") from the centre back; sew directly in the fold closest to the staystitching, gently coaxing the bias strip to lie smoothly around the curve (no manhandling or pulling, just encouragement).

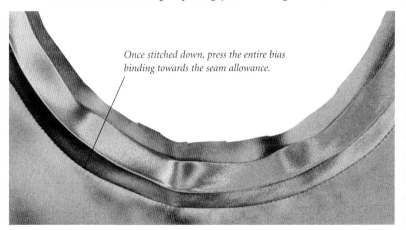

Once stitched down, press the entire bias binding towards the seam allowance.

5. Join the binding ends

Stop stitching about 2.5cm (1") from the centre back. Determine where the two ends will meet at the centre back and join them in a seam on the straight grain. Trim the seam allowances to 6mm (¼") and press open. Finish stitching the last bit of the binding to the garment.

Pressing double-fold bias

1. Fold the strip in half lengthways, right side out, and press.

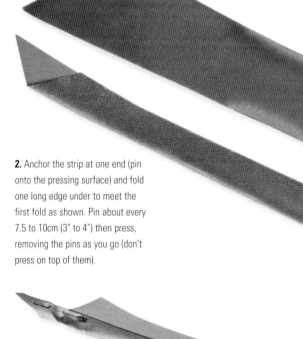

2. Anchor the strip at one end (pin onto the pressing surface) and fold one long edge under to meet the first fold as shown. Pin about every 7.5 to 10cm (3" to 4") then press, removing the pins as you go (don't press on top of them).

3. Repeat the process for the other edge of the strip, but this time don't bring the cut edge all the way to the first fold – you want one side of the bias to be a little wider than the other. A difference of 2mm (¹⁄₁₆") is ideal.

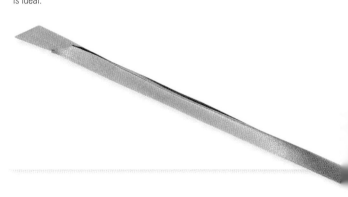

6. Trim away the seam allowance

Trim away the garment neckline seam allowance, cutting off the staystitching as you do this.

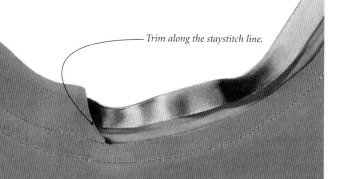

Trim along the staystitch line.

7. The trimmed seam allowance

Be sure to cut neatly so the new edge is smooth and an even distance from the seam that attaches the binding. This is extremely important because the binding will wrap the edge, so you want that edge to be smooth. Also, on some finer fabrics, the staystitching can form a very unattractive bumpy ridge – so make sure you cut it off!

8. Wrap and pin the binding

Fold the binding up and over the edge to the wrong side and pin it in place. This is the only time I find pinning necessary in this process. Make sure the binding covers the stitches on the inside of the garment. If your folded bias binding does not extend below the seamline by 2mm (1/16"), go back and evenly trim away a small amount more from the seam allowance.

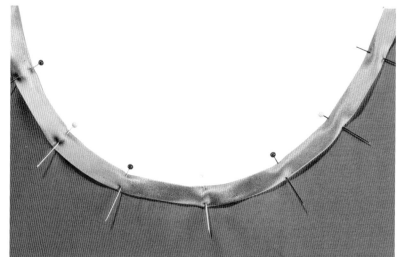

Joining bias strips

If you are working with scraps or small amounts of fabric and can't cut a bias strip in the length you need, join two pieces on the straight grain.

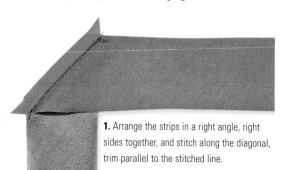

1. Arrange the strips in a right angle, right sides together, and stitch along the diagonal, trim parallel to the stitched line.

2. Press the seam allowances open.

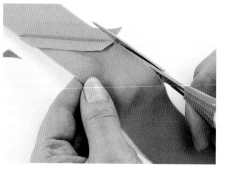

3. Trim the extending corner to make a neat edge.

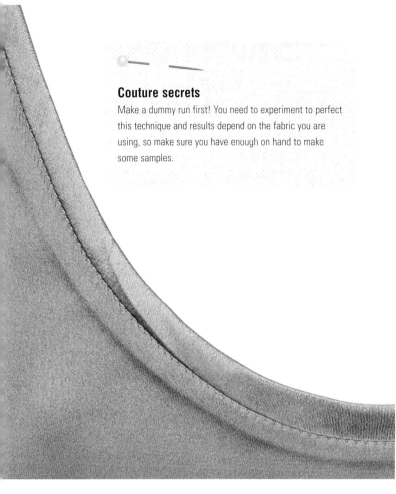

Couture secrets

Make a dummy run first! You need to experiment to perfect this technique and results depend on the fabric you are using, so make sure you have enough on hand to make some samples.

STYLE SUGGESTION

- Introducing a complementary texture when selecting an accent colour for the binding completes the look.

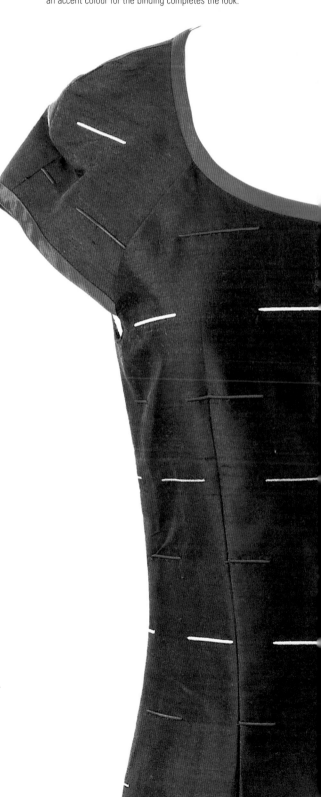

9. Complete the binding

Stitch in the ditch (just below the previous seamline) from the right side, using a topstitch foot or an edgestitch foot. Remove the pins as you go.

By stitching from the right side, you can see that your stitches fall in the ditch of the previous seam. You should catch the reverse of the binding as you go, since you left an overlap.

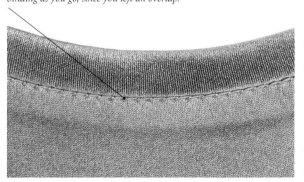

DOUBLE-FOLD BINDING ON CHIFFON

Chiffon! Now there is a word that will conjure up fear and trepidation in the most experienced sewer. Finishing the edges of anything made from chiffon – feminine, semi-transparent ethereal garments – can be a daunting task. But silk organza comes to the rescue; if you use it to stabilize the edge, it keeps the chiffon in order. Here is a way to add a charmeuse binding to chiffon.

SEWING TOOLS AND MATERIALS

- Silk organza, natural colour, for neckline interfacing
- Microtex or sharp needle, recommended
- Single-hole throat plate, recommended
- Straight-stitch foot
- Topstitch foot

STABILIZE THE NECKLINE

1. Interface the neckline

Cut a piece of silk organza the shape of the neckline for each garment piece, making it about twice the width of the seam allowance. Pin or hand-tack in place in the neck seam allowance.

2. Stitch along the seamline

Staystitch the entire neckline directly on the seamline using a regular stitch length setting of 2.5mm (10 stitches per inch).

PREPARE THE BINDING

3. Cut and fold the bias strip

Follow steps 2 and 3 of Double-Fold Silk Charmeuse Binding, page 30, to cut a bias strip and fold it to the right size for the binding.

ATTACH THE BINDING

4. Position and stitch in place

Follow step 4 of Double-Fold Silk Charmeuse Binding, page 31, to sew the binding onto the right side of the garment.

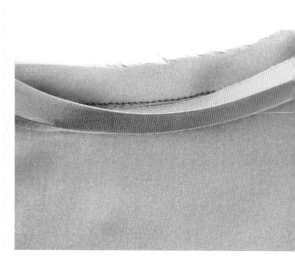

5. Trim away the seam allowance

Trim away the garment neckline seam allowance, cutting off the staystitching as you do this. Be sure to cut neatly so the new edge is smooth and an even distance from the seam that attaches the binding.

Trim the organza extending below the seam that attaches the binding, cutting about 2mm (¹⁄₁₆") from the stitches. This small extension will support the final topstitching.

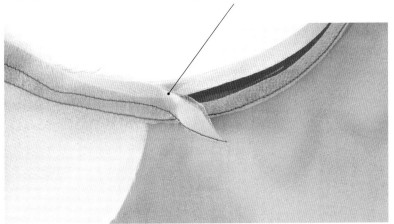

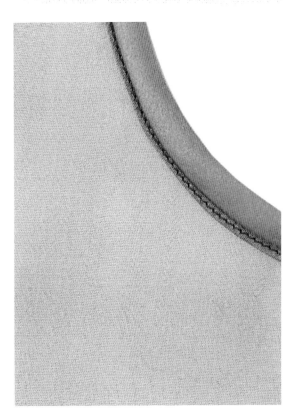

Couture secret

'Natural' – meaning a beige or ecru tone – is a good colour choice for the organza because some will remain in the garment and natural will not change the colour of the chiffon it backs. If you are dark-skinned, a colour closer to your skin tone may work better.

Note

- Besides reinforcing the curves and providing support inside the binding, the silk organza is a big help for managing the chiffon.

6. Wrap and pin the binding

Follow step 8 of Double-Fold Silk Charmeuse Binding, page 32, to wrap the binding over the neckline edge and pin it in place.

7. Complete the binding

Stitch in the ditch (just below the previous seamline) from the right side, using a topstitch foot. Remove the pins as you go.

Free-flow Charmeuse Binding on Chiffon

This is an innovative method for hemming chiffon. Double-fold silk charmeuse binding is employed to provide an artfully clean finish for the hem while adding a subtle shimmer of light and movement.

- Tissue paper may be helpful

PREPARE THE BINDING

1. Preparing the binding

Following the directions on pages 30–31, prepare double-fold silk charmeuse binding.

ATTACH THE BINDING

2. Place the binding and stitch

Lay the garment right side up on a flat surface. Arrange the binding in the desired shape near the hemline. The raw edge of the binding should face the bottom (hemline) of the garment. Pin in place and stitch. Tissue paper placed between the fabric and the feed dogs may be helpful for this part. Complete the application of the binding, following the steps on pages 32–33.

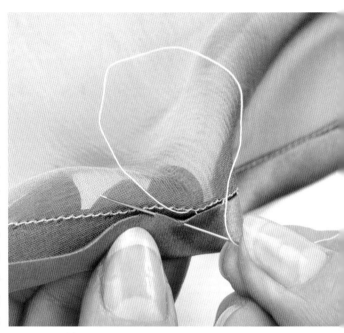

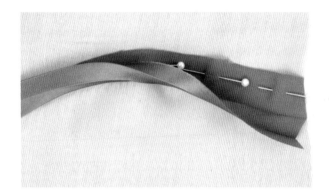

FINAL STITCHING

3. Completing the final stitching

The final stitching should be done by hand.

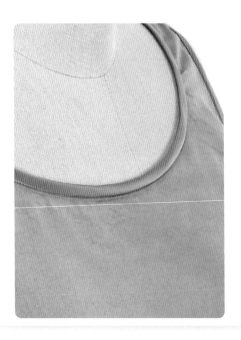

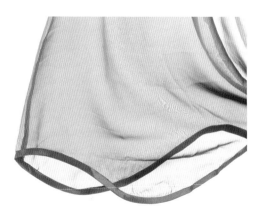

STYLE SUGGESTION

- Left: The subtle shimmer of colour is the icing on the cake.
- Centre: The finished free-flow binding on chiffon.
- Right: The binding adds a hint of femininity to this traditional stripe and emphasizes the curves.

PIPED DOUBLE-FOLD BINDING

It is always a good idea to experiment with a variety of banding and binding techniques to determine which is best suited to the fabric at hand and gives you the look you want. This is the twin-sister technique to Double-Fold Silk Charmeuse Binding on page 30. Charmeuse is so fluid, it's tricky to handle, but when your fabric is more stable, this technique will produce a similar effect with a lot less effort. For a bit of fun, this version of the binding is a variation of the traditional technique: It's applied 'backwards' – sewn first to the wrong side of the garment, and then wrapped to the front, with piping tucked under the edge on the right side – and has a more artful, whimsical look.

- Prepared piping 3mm (⅛") a bit more than enough to go around neckline

- Cording foot, optional

PREPARE THE BINDING
2–3. Cut and fold the bias strip
Follow steps 2 and 3 of Double-Fold Silk Charmeuse Binding, page 30, to cut a bias strip and fold it to the right size for the binding.

STABILIZE THE NECKLINE
1. Stitch along the seamline
Follow step 1 of Double-Fold Silk Charmeuse Binding, page 30, to staystitch the neckline.

Attach the binding

4. Position and stitch in place

Place the garment wrong side up. Open the folded bias strip and place it right side down on the garment, with the end at the centre back neckline; position it so the strip lies on the garment side of the staystitching and the cut edge of the narrower side is aligned against the staystitching as shown. Begin stitching about 2.5cm (1") from the centre back; sew directly in the fold closest to the staystitching, gently coaxing the bias strip to lie smoothly around the curve (no man-handling or pulling, just encouragement).

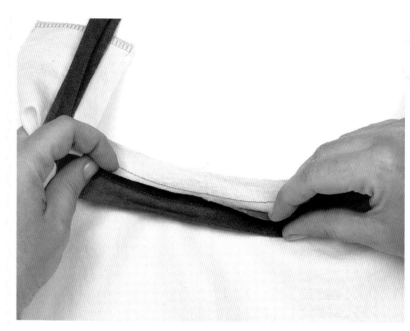

5. Trim the seam allowances

Stop stitching 2.5cm (1") from the centre back. Determine where the two ends will meet at the centre back and join them in a seam on the straight grain. Trim the seam allowances to 6mm (¼") and press open. Finish stitching the last bit of the binding to the garment. Follow step 6 of Double-Fold Silk Charmeuse Binding, page 32, to trim the neckline seam allowance.

6. Prepare for the piping

The binding has been turned to the front of the garment and pressed in place. The neckline is now ready for the piping to be added.

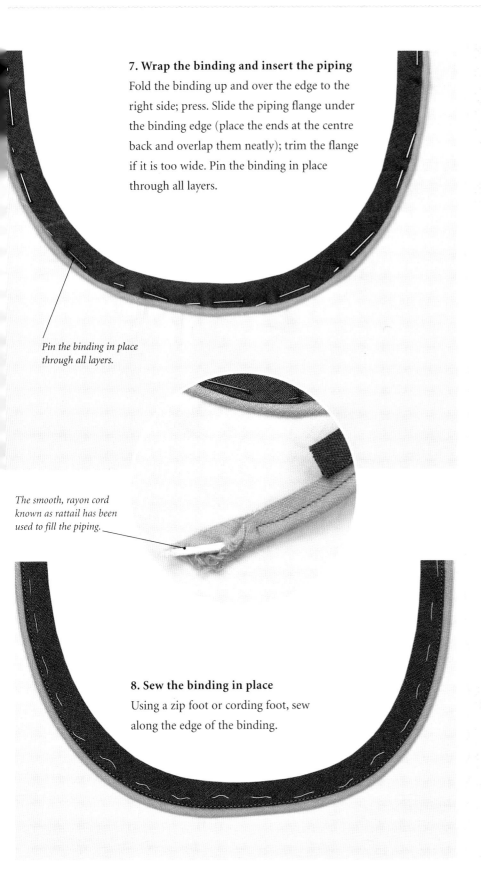

7. Wrap the binding and insert the piping

Fold the binding up and over the edge to the right side; press. Slide the piping flange under the binding edge (place the ends at the centre back and overlap them neatly); trim the flange if it is too wide. Pin the binding in place through all layers.

Pin the binding in place through all layers.

The smooth, rayon cord known as rattail has been used to fill the piping.

8. Sew the binding in place

Using a zip foot or cording foot, sew along the edge of the binding.

Couture secret

This is where a cording foot is a wonderful help. Centre the foot over the piping and position the needle so that it will stitch through the binding close to the piping.

Style Suggestion

• Any decorative trim that has a flange may be used instead of piping.

Couture secret

It's helpful to hand-tack all in place at this point. There are several layers at play and too many opportunities for shifting when everything is stitched in place.

SINGLE-FOLD BINDING ON KNIT FABRIC

The following technique is a mainstay for knit edges: necklines, armholes or hemlines. A tee or vest top should be effortless to wear, comfortable, and require minimal care. Facings are not a part of this profile. Something a bit cleaner that does not make an unscheduled appearance is preferable. This technique emulates the expensive designer tee or vest top that is made with specialized equipment.

- Fusible interfacing for knits: This allows the knit to retain some stretch for comfort.

- Foot designed to sew knits, recommended

- Topstitch foot, recommended

STABILIZE THE NECKLINE

1. Interface the neckline

Cut a strip of fusible interfacing the shape of the neckline for each garment piece, making it the width of the seam allowance plus 1cm (⅜"). Fuse each strip to the wrong side of its piece, positioning it so that it covers the seam allowance. This will stabilize the area and facilitate smoother topstitching.

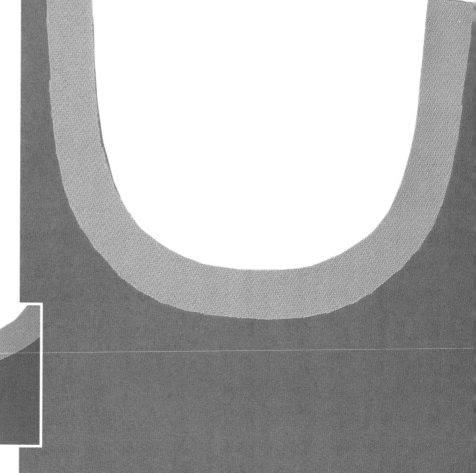

Back

PREPARE THE BINDING
3. Cut the neckband strip

Sew the shoulder seams and press open. Measure
the length of the entire neckline and add 10cm (4").
Cut a strip this length and 3.5cm (1⅜") wide on the
crossways grain of the knit fabric – so that the stretch
runs the length of the band. This makes it easier
to apply the band to the back neckline curve.
If you wish, overlock one long edge for a
more professional look.

Back

2. Stitch along the seamline

Staystitch the entire neckline
directly on the seamline using
a stitch length setting of 2.5mm
(10 stitches per inch).

*Staystitch the neckline
on the seam.*

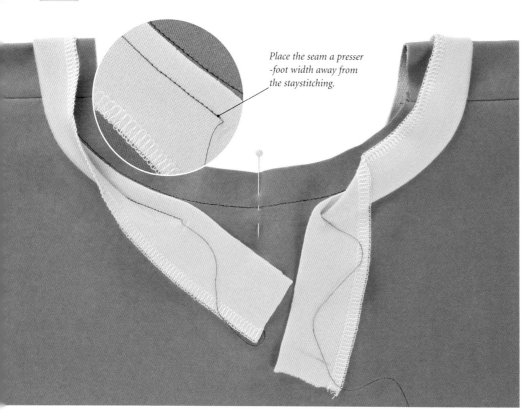

Place the seam a presser-foot width away from the staystitching.

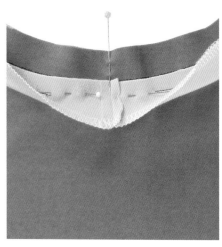

5. Join the binding ends

Determine where the two tails will meet at the centre back and join them in a seam. Trim the seam allowances to 6mm (¼") and press open. Finish stitching the last bit of the binding to the garment.

ATTACH THE BINDING

4. Position and stitch in place

Mark the centre back of the neckline with a pin (most vest tops and tees do not have a centre back seam). Beginning at the centre back and leaving a 7.5cm (3")-long tail, place the binding and garment right sides together, aligning the unfinished edge of the binding with the staystitching as shown. Begin stitching about 2.5cm (1") from the centre back, placing the seam a presser-foot width away from the staystitching/binding edge – a healthy 6mm (¼") away from the edge. As you sew, stretch the binding just enough to encourage it to hug the curve. Stop stitching about 2.5cm (1") from the centre back.

Note
• Because each fabric stretches differently, you can't sew the binding into a ring before attaching it to the neckline.

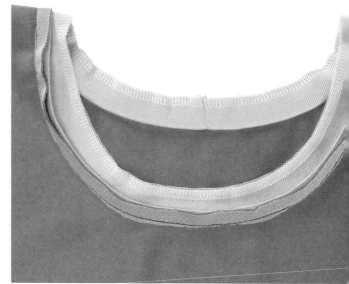

6. Press and trim the neckline

Trim away the seam allowance on the garment, cutting off the staystitching, which can create an unsightly ridge if left on. Press the seam as sewn to embed the stitches, then press the binding and seam allowances away from the garment.

7. Pin and topstitch the binding

Wrap the binding around the remaining seam allowance (it should extend below the seam on the wrong side of the garment) and pin in place. From the right side of the garment, stitch in the ditch (see glossary, page 156) through all thicknesses.

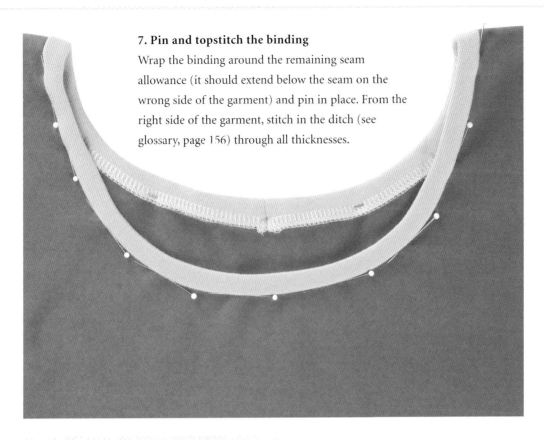

Note

• Where there is an intersecting seam, for instance at the shoulder, it may be necessary to trim away a bit more due to the added thickness.

The 'v-snip' is a layering technique used to reduce bulk.

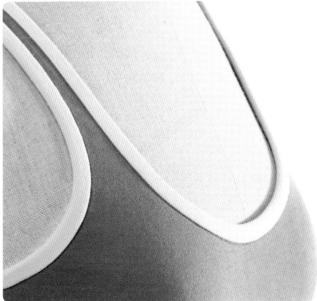

Style suggestion

• You can experiment with contrasting colours and textures when using this binding.

BABY FRENCH BINDING

This simple, clean finish is really a skinny bias facing that's secured from the right side with a twin needle. It's useful on lightweight, ethereal tops and for layered looks. It is ideal for handkerchief linen and other lightweight woven fabrics such as voile, batiste, organdy and China silk.

For the binding, use very lightweight cotton batiste in a colour that matches your garment fabric. Because the binding acts as a facing and is not meant to be seen, a contrast colour could detract from its simplicity. (A contrast colour is used here for teaching purposes.)

- Cotton batiste, for binding
- Twin needle
- Wooden seam stick, for pressing
- Tissue paper (optional)

STABILIZE THE NECKLINE

1. Stitch along the seamline

Sew the shoulder seams and press the allowances open. Staystitch the entire neckline directly on the seamline using a stitch length setting of 2.5mm (10 stitches per inch). If your fabric is so thin that it wobbles when stitched, place a single layer of tissue paper between it and the feed dogs as a temporary stabilizer.

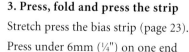

Here you can see the decrease in width after the bias strip was stretch-pressed.

PREPARE THE BINDING

2. Cut the bias strip

Measure the length of the entire neckline and add 10cm (4"); this is the length to cut the strip. To find the width, double the seam allowance depth, add 1.25cm (½") and add a bit more to account for shrinkage when you stretch-press the band (see page 23). The amount to add varies from 3mm to 1cm (⅛" to ⅜") depending on the fabric. Cut a bias strip of the required size.

3. Press, fold and press the strip

Stretch press the bias strip (page 23). Press under 6mm (¼") on one end of the strip. Then fold the strip in half lengthways, right side out, and press again.

ATTACH THE BINDING

4. Position and stitch in place

Place the garment right side up. Position the bias strip on top, beginning at the centre back with the end that has been folded under and aligning the cut edges of the bias with the neckline edge. Begin stitching about 2.5cm (1") from the centre back, stitching exactly on the staystitching. As you sew, manipulate the binding so that it follows the curve but do not stretch it.

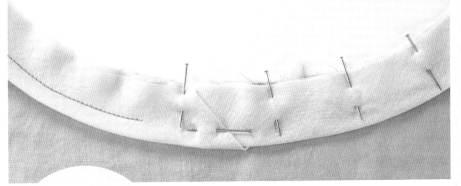

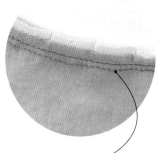

Clip the seam allowances along the curve.

5. Join the binding end

Stop stitching about 2.5cm (1") from the centre back. Determine where the two ends will meet at the centre back and join them in a seam or lap them (slide the raw end inside the pressed end) on the straight grain, using the pressed under edge as a stitching guide. Trim the seam allowances to 6mm (¼") and press open. Finish stitching the last of the binding to the garment. Trim the seam allowance on the garment neckline to 3mm (⅛") and on the binding to a scant 6mm (¼"). Carefully clip the allowances along the entire curve.

Note

- Because each fabric stretches differently, you can't sew the binding into a ring before attaching it to the neckline. Now is the time to check and make sure that your band is an even width all the way around the neckline.

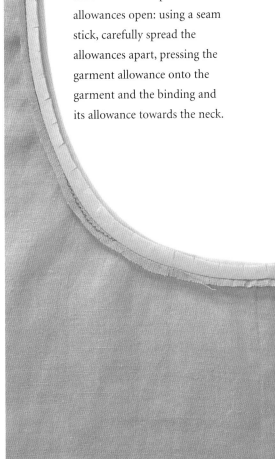

6. Press the seam

Press the seam as sewn to embed the stitches. Now press the seam allowances open: using a seam stick, carefully spread the allowances apart, pressing the garment allowance onto the garment and the binding and its allowance towards the neck.

7. Pin and topstitch the binding

Fold the binding to the wrong side of the garment; press and pin in place. Using a twin needle, topstitch from the right side of the garment through all thicknesses.

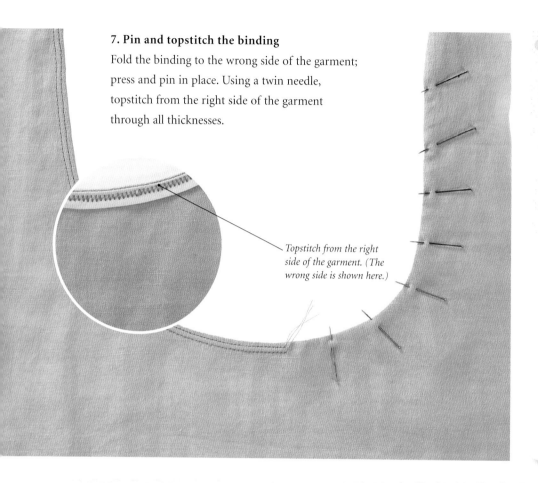

Topstitch from the right side of the garment. (The wrong side is shown here.)

Couture Secret

Because the binding will be folded down as a facing, pressing the allowances open may seem like a lot of fuss (and it is!), but the pay-off is huge. This seemingly insignificant step allows the final pressing to be more crisp, neater and much more accurate.

Alternative joining method

Joining the ends of the bias with a seam works well on stable fabrics. When working with soft, drapey fabrics such as charmeuse and chiffon, there is an easier, more practical method: begin stitching at the pressed-under end, and when you reach the other end, simply lay the unpressed end on top of the stitched end for about 1.25cm (½"). Stitch and then cut off the excess.

Single-Fold Binding on Chiffon

To give chiffon a polished finish with just a touch of dimension, make a narrow self-binding. As with the Double-Fold Charmeuse Binding on Chiffon, begin by supporting the edge with silk organza. You'll need the same supplies as for those techniques.

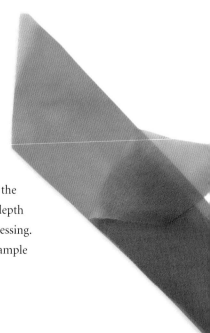

STABILIZE THE NECKLINE

Follow steps 1 and 2 from Double-Fold Charmeuse Binding On Chiffon, page 34, to cut organza and staystitch it to the neckline.

PREPARE AND ATTACH THE BINDING

Follow steps 2 and 3 of Baby French Binding, page 44, but use this formula for the binding width: twice the seam allowance depth plus 2.5cm (1") plus enough for stretch pressing. Read the directions through and make a sample to find the right width.

ATTACH THE BINDING

Follow steps 4 and 5 of Baby French Binding (pages 44–45) but in step 5, do not clip the seam allowances. Then trim the organza extending below the seam that attaches the binding, cutting about 2mm (¹⁄₁₆") from the stitches. This small extension will support the final stitching. Wrap and fold the binding up and over the edge to the wrong side and stitch in the ditch from the right side or sew it in place by hand for a softer look.

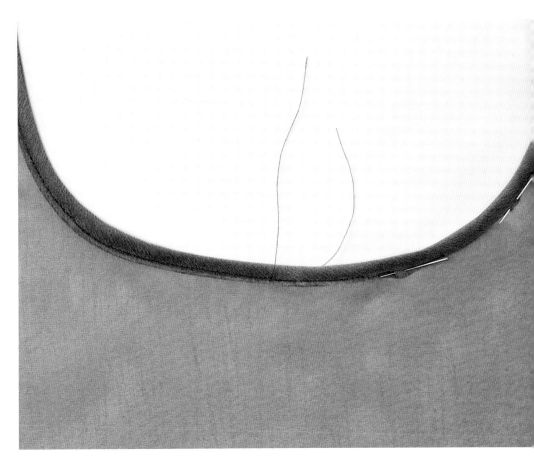

Baby French Binding on Chiffon

If you'd like a clean simple finish, you can finish chiffon with a baby French binding – like the Baby French Binding on page 44 – if you support the edge with silk organza as in the Double-Fold Charmeuse Binding on Chiffon on page 34. You'll need the same supplies as for the latter technique.

STABILIZE THE NECKLINE

Follow steps 1 and 2 from Double-Fold Charmeuse Binding On Chiffon, page 34, to cut organza and staystitch it to the neckline.

Couture secret

It can be challenging to cut bias strips of chiffon, and tissue paper can be a very helpful assistant for this. Place one layer of tissue beneath the chiffon and a second layer on top. This sandwich stabilizes the fabric for optimal accuracy while you cut.

MAKE AND ATTACH THE BINDING

From this point, follow the directions for Baby French
Binding, page 44, beginning with step 2. Here are the
points of difference:

*Because chiffon is so light and drapey,
add a bit more width when you cut
the bias. Read the directions through
and make a sample to find the
right width.*

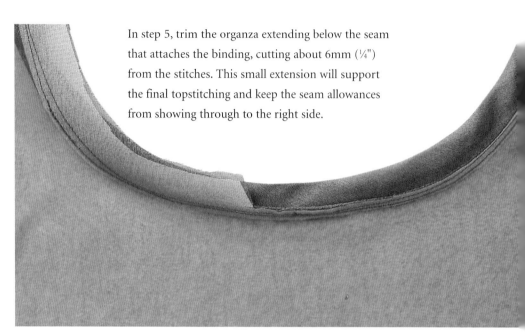

In step 5, trim the organza extending below the seam
that attaches the binding, cutting about 6mm (¼")
from the stitches. This small extension will support
the final topstitching and keep the seam allowances
from showing through to the right side.

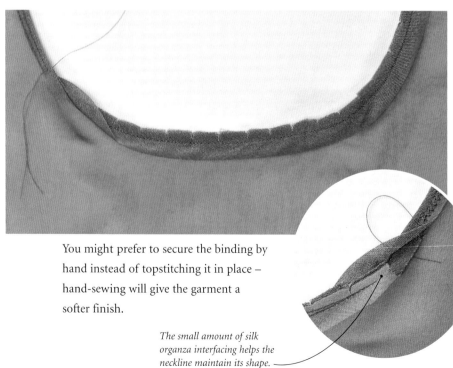

You might prefer to secure the binding by
hand instead of topstitching it in place –
hand-sewing will give the garment a
softer finish.

*The small amount of silk
organza interfacing helps the
neckline maintain its shape.*

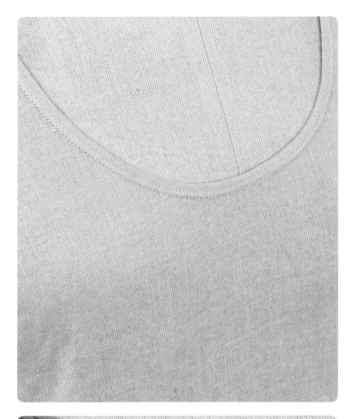

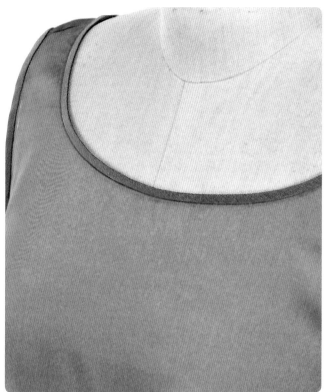

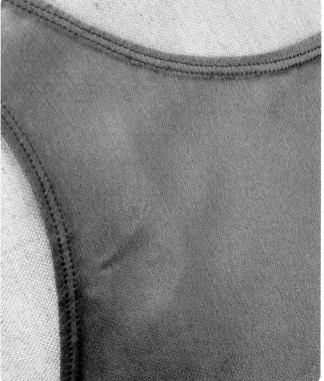

Style suggestions

- Top left: Baby French Binding on linen acts as an effective facing.
- Top right: Charmeuse was used here to bind the chiffon and to introduce an accent colour.
- Bottom left: The same 'binding-as-facing' approach was used here as with the chiffon.

CHAPTER TWO

DESIGN DETAILS: ON SHOW

The following techniques are basic ideas, or suggestions for showcasing individuality and creativity. The classic, gored pencil-line skirt has been accented to emphasize the vertical seaming so flattering on all women. Charmeuse ribbons enhance the waistline in a pleasing, slimming way. Cuffs and collars offer yet another canvas for design details such as channel stitching and cording. Hopefully, these techniques and ideas will serve to propel you forwards to a fresh, innovative design experience.

Finishing touches

It's all in the details. Beautifully realized
finishing touches emphasize and underscore
couture garments.

*Valentino Prêt-à-Porter Spring/Summer 2010
Show, Paris Fashion Week*

CHANNEL-STITCHED ACCENTS

Silk charmeuse is one of the most luxurious fabrics with a sensuous hand and drape. When backed with cotton flannel it becomes more stable, easier to handle and heavier. All these characteristics are nice for garment sections that are fitted rather than fluid, for instance a bodice, or that benefit from weight, such as a hemline that isn't meant to flutter. Securing the charmeuse to the flannel with rows of parallel stitches (known as channel stitching) ensures that the layers handle as one and adds a decorative detail, too.

SEWING TOOLS AND MATERIALS

- Cotton flannel to back channel-stitched areas

- Walking foot or roller foot, optional

CHANNEL STITCH THE FABRIC

1. Cut the fabric

Decide which sections of the garment you wish to channel stitch. For each pattern piece you need, cut a piece of charmeuse and a piece of flannel slightly larger than needed.

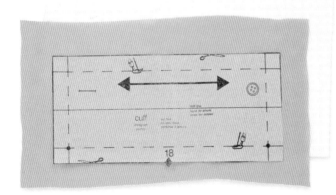

2. Tack the layers together

Lay the charmeuse right side up on the flannel, aligning the edges. Sew them together along one long edge and two short edges. This allows the stitches to draw up independently as necessary when stitched.

Notes

- Channel stitching may cause the fabric to draw up slightly, so cut the charmeuse and flannel a bit larger than needed for each pattern piece before layering the two fabrics and stitching them together.

- When cutting the pieces to be channel stitched, cut rectangles, with the lengthways grain orientated to reflect the grain of the garment section; you'll cut the exact shape from each pattern piece after stitching.

- It may be easier to cut your garment if you purchase a bit more fabric than specified on the pattern directions.

MAKE THE GARMENT

4. Cut out the garment

When fabric has been channel stitched, cut out the appropriate pattern piece.

5. Sew the garment

Follow your pattern directions to make the garment.

3. Channel stitch the fabric

Sew the fabrics together with parallel rows of stitches; the spacing and direction of the rows is up to you. Usually, a distance the width of the presser foot works well. Use a stitch length of 3mm (8 stitches per inch). Press with an organza press cloth after channel stitching.

Completed rectangle of channel-stitched fabric.

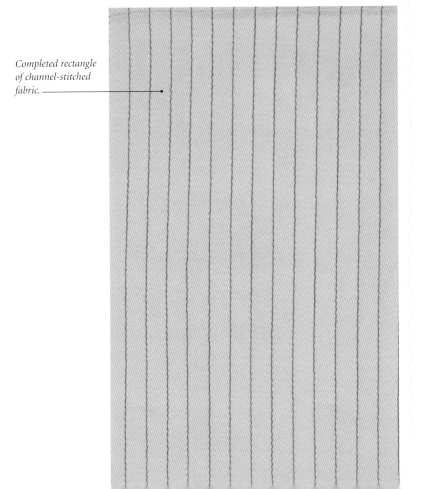

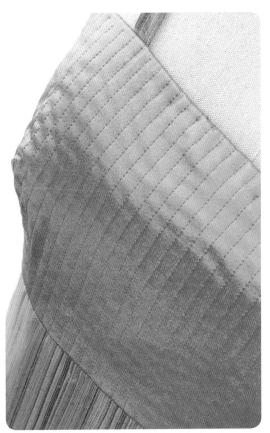

Style suggestion

- Flannel, channel-stitched behind the charmeuse made it possible to sculpt the bodice of this dress so that it smoothly conforms to the curves of the body.

CORDED ACCENTS

When cording is placed beneath the face fabric, subtle textural changes take place, adding depth and surface design to the garment. This interesting designer touch can be applied to collars, cuffs or hembands.

Using a cording foot can help when creating this effect because it has a groove on the bottom which holds the cord in place while sewing. A twin needle straddles the cord and secures it in place without stitching through it. Pintuck feet have several grooves on the bottom, allowing for closer spacing of the cords.

SEWING TOOLS AND MATERIALS

- Silk organza to back corded areas
- Soft yarn or cord of your choice, for the fill (the samples show a fine, soft wool yarn)
- 3-groove pintuck foot
- Twin needle

Notes

- Adding the cording may cause the fabric to draw up slightly, so cut the fashion fabric and organza a bit larger than needed for each pattern piece before layering the two fabrics and stitching them together.
- When cutting the pieces to be corded, just cut rectangles, with the lengthways grain appropriately orientated relative to the placement of the pattern piece; you'll cut the exact shape from each pattern piece after the stitching is done.
- It may be easier to cut your garment if you purchase a bit more fabric than specified on the pattern directions.
- If you place the first cord right against the tacking stitches you'll find it difficult to sew the pieces together later.

PREPARE THE FABRIC AND FILL

1. Cut the fabric

Decide which sections of the garment you wish to cord. For each pattern piece you need, cut a piece of fashion fabric and a piece of silk organza slightly larger than needed.

2. Tack the layers together

Lay the fashion fabric right side up on the organza, aligning the edges. Sew them together along one long edge.

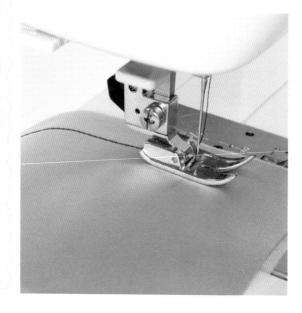

3. Cut the fill

Decide how many rows of cord you want to incorporate. For each, cut a piece of your chosen cord a bit longer than the edge to be corded. You may choose to experiment with cords or string of varying thickness and rigidity. Each fabric will behave differently with the various 'fills'. Mousetail and rattail produce a more pronounced ridge than string, but there is greater difficulty manipulating and seaming the garment sections. It is always wise to make a small sample first to determine the overall look you desire. Here, soft yarn is used.

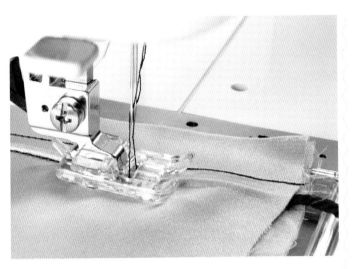

CORD THE FABRIC

4. Sew in the first piece of cord

Attach the 3-groove pintuck foot and twin needle
to your machine. Slide a length of cord between the
fabric layers, aligning it parallel to the tacked edge and
about 6mm (¼") from the stitches. Place the fabric
right side up in the machine, with the stitches to the
left of the foot and the cord between the two needles.
Stitch along the cord.

5. Continue to cord the fabric

Place the second length of yarn next to the first,
positioning it between the needles, and stitch in place.
Repeat to add as many lengths as you like.

MAKE THE GARMENT

6. Cut out the garment

When fabric has been corded cut out the appropriate
pattern piece.

7. Sew the garment

Follow your pattern directions to make the garment.

Style suggestion

- This vintage evening gown has a corded collar, and corded flanges
  on both shoulders. The flanges are simple rectangles that substitute
  for sleeves. The collar was corded along the long edge first. A
  second layer of organza was added to support more cording along
  the front edge of the collar.

Petersham 'Peek' Seam

Rethink the classic pencil skirt by adding a trim to the side-front seams. If you construct the skirt with flat-felled seams it's easy to slip a length of ribbon into each. The result is an updated wardrobe staple with new vitality. When you cut the skirt, make the seam allowances 2cm (¾") deep; they'll be easier to handle and make a bigger statement. Check the recommended seam allowance on the pattern first, though – you may need to adjust it.

SEWING TOOLS AND MATERIALS

- Petersham or grosgrain ribbon or similar flat trim, 3.75cm (½") wide, enough to embellish the chosen seams.

BEGIN THE FLAT-FELLED SEAM

1. Sew the skirt pieces together
Place the pieces to be joined wrong sides together. Sew each seam with a 2cm (¾") allowance.

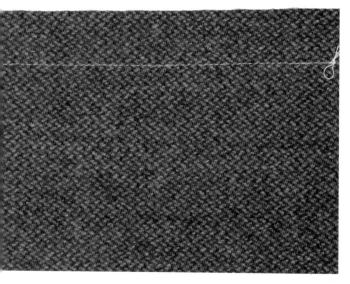

2. Press and trim the seam
Press the work as sewn to embed the stitches, then press the seam allowances open. Decide which way the flat-felled seam will fold (usually away from the centre panel). Trim the allowance to be covered to 3mm (⅛").

3. Position the top allowance
Press the wide, untrimmed seam allowance over the trimmed seam allowance.

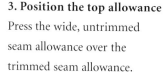

Note
- Repeat the steps that follow on all seams you wish to embellish.

4. Prepare the allowance edge

Fold under the raw edge of the top seam allowance and press; make sure to fold under an even amount so that the remaining allowance is a constant width.

The original seam stitching is visible and the opposite side has been folded and pressed.

EMBELLISH THE SEAM

5. Cut and insert the ribbon

Cut a length of ribbon equal to the flat-felled seam length. Slide it under the top seam allowance, positioning to extend evenly along the seam. Pin or tack the ribbon in place and topstitch near the folded edge of the allowance through all thicknesses.

Petersham 'Peek' on a Wrap Skirt

If you'd like to embellish the loose edge of a wrap skirt (or a fake wrap) to look like the trimmed flat-felled seams on the pencil skirt, it's very easy. If you're making a fake wrap skirt, be sure to embellish the edge before joining the overlapped panels at the waist.

EMBELLISH THE SKIRT EDGE

1. Attach and press the ribbon

Cut a length of ribbon equal to the skirt edge. Place the ribbon and skirt edge right sides together, edges aligned; sew. Press the work as sewn to embed the stitches. Then press the seam allowances towards the body of the skirt so that the ribbon extends away from it.

The skirt edge (seam allowances) from the reverse side.

2. Tack the layer

Tack the layers of fabric together
at the waistline.

*The wrapped panel
extends over the
underneath section
of the garment.*

Style suggestion

- This wool/cashmere pencil skirt is accented with a
  Petersham 'peek' at the edge of the flat-felled
  seams, emphasizing the graceful, body-conscious
  lines of the skirt.

HONG KONG FINISH ON THE OUTSIDE

This traditional method of finishing seam allowances with a binding is known as the Hong Kong finish. It is labour-intensive and therefore usually reserved for high-end garments. This fresh variation places the finished seam allowances on the outside of the garment; it's a nice way to emphasize line and add texture. For this technique, the wrong side of the fabric is exposed in the seam allowances, so use a reversible fabric or one with a wrong side that you like. This finish is not suitable for curved seams for which the allowances need to be clipped to lie flat.

SEWING TOOLS AND MATERIALS

- Topstitching foot, recommended
- Fabric for bias strips for seam binding, type and amount depend on your project
- Organza press cloth, to keep the fabric from glazing

PREPARE THE BIAS STRIPS

1. Cut the bias strips

Cut enough 3.75cm (1½")-wide bias strips to bind the edges of all the seam allowances that you wish to finish. Because the joins in pieced strips would be glaring, make sure that you have enough fabric to make long, unpieced strips. The extra width of the strips makes the process easier and can be trimmed away later.

2. Press the bias strips

Stretch press the strips (see page 23).

BIND THE SEAM ALLOWANCE EDGE

3. Sew on the bias strips

Place a garment section wrong side up. Lay a bias strip, right side down, along the edge to be bound. Sew in place, stitching 6mm (¼") from the edge (the width of your presser foot).

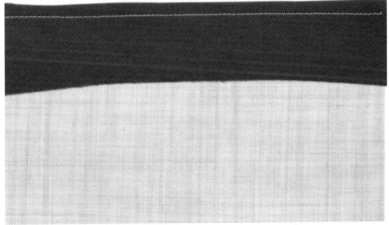

Note
- The binding is applied to the seam allowances before the garment is constructed, so it is imperative to make a fitting toile (see page 154) and correct your pattern as needed before beginning. Seams finished in this manner should not be altered.

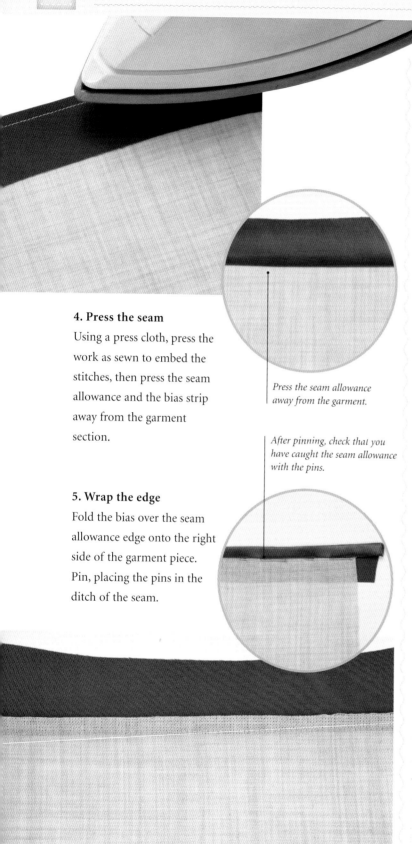

4. Press the seam

Using a press cloth, press the work as sewn to embed the stitches, then press the seam allowance and the bias strip away from the garment section.

Press the seam allowance away from the garment.

After pinning, check that you have caught the seam allowance with the pins.

5. Wrap the edge

Fold the bias over the seam allowance edge onto the right side of the garment piece. Pin, placing the pins in the ditch of the seam.

6. Sew the binding in place

With the garment section wrong side up, stitch in the ditch to secure the binding.

7. Trim the excess bias

Turn the piece over. Trim the bias strip about 3mm (⅛") from the stitching.

Notes

• Try using prints, checks or bold colours for the binding fabric. Have fun!

• Repeat the steps in this section on all edges to be bound.

ASSEMBLE THE GARMENT

8. Sew the garment seams

Refer to your pattern directions for the construction
sequence. For each seam, place the garment pieces wrong
sides together, aligning the bound edges. Pin and then
stitch each seam.

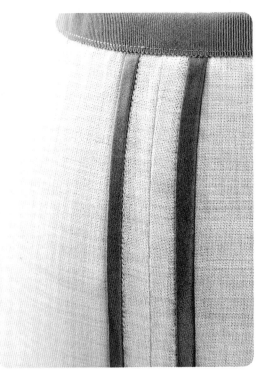

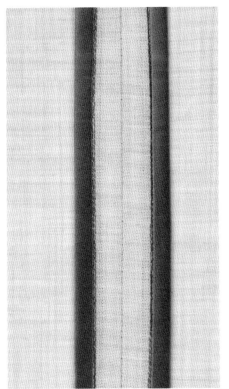

9. Press the garment seams

Press the work as sewn to
embed the stitches, then press
the seam allowances open. On
each allowance, stitch in the
ditch over previous stitching
through all thicknesses.

10. Complete the garment

Follow your pattern directions
to complete the garment.

Style suggestion

• This seven-gore pencil skirt is made of lightweight
  wool with an accent of contrasting silk charmeuse.

WIDE CHARMEUSE HEM BAND

This method of finishing a hem is decorative as well as functional. The subtle shimmer of the charmeuse looks a bit like frosting on a cake, and the band lends weight to the bottom of the garment. Plus there is the opportunity to experiment with colour combinations.

- Topstitch foot
- Silk charmeuse, enough for the hem band

PREPARING THE BAND

1. Cutting the strip

Cut a strip of charmeuse twice the desired width, plus 18mm (¾"). The strip should be long enough to follow the hemline with extra for joining. The strip may be cut on the crossways grain unless the hem is curved. (That would require a bias strip.)

2. Folding and pressing the strip

Fold the strip in half along its length and press. Machine-tack the raw edges together for ease of handling.

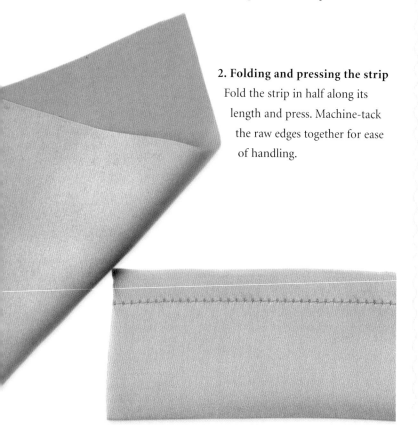

ATTACHING THE BAND

3. Position and stitch in place

Place the band on the wrong side of the garment with raw edges aligned. Stitch, using a 1cm (⅜") seam allowance.

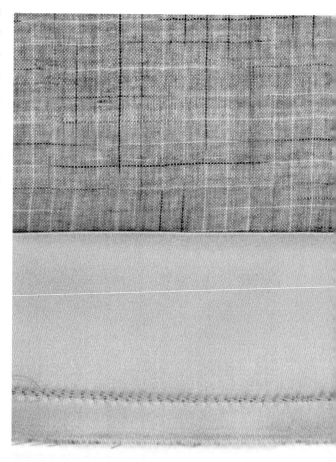

4. Press the seam

Press to embed the stitches. Now, very carefully, press the seam open. Although it is tempting, do not overlook this step. A neater fold and a nicer-looking band are worth this added fuss!

The finished hemline features silk banding on the face and no raw edges on the inside of the garment.

5. Finish stitching the band

Fold the band to the right side of the garment and topstitch through all the thicknesses near the top edge of the band, about 2mm (¹⁄₁₆") in from the edge.

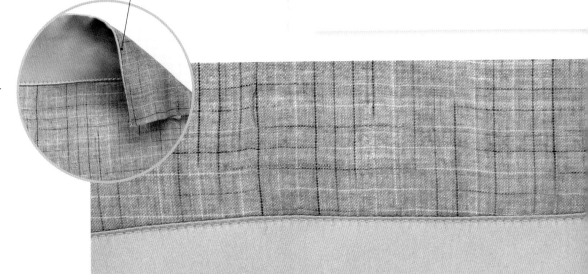

Style suggestion

- The silk banding on the hem of this floaty sheer skirt adds weight to the hem of the garment as well as providing an attractive design feature.

RIBBON-TRIMMED HEM

This clever manoeuvre gives a neat, clean finish and is often used on sheer fabrics. The ribbon adds stability and definition to the hemline and nicely finishes the inside, too. It adds a whimsical, carefree element to the garment and invites experimentation. Try decorative ribbons such as plaids, stripes or dots.

SEWING TOOLS AND MATERIALS

- Ribbon trim

ATTACHING THE RIBBON

1. Place and stitch
With wrong sides together, align the edge of the ribbon with the raw edge of the garment. Stitch close to the edge of the ribbon farthest from the raw edge of the garment.

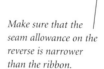

Make sure that the seam allowance on the reverse is narrower than the ribbon.

3. Finish stitching the ribbon
Press the ribbon to the front of the garment and topstitch the remaining edge of the ribbon through all thicknesses.

2. Trim the seam allowance
Trim away the garment seam allowance so it is slightly narrower than the ribbon.

Style suggestion
- The ribbon selection for this hem makes the print 'pop' and adds weight and movement.

DECORATIVE TRIM HEM

This is another hemming technique that applies trim with no added bulk and finishes the inside of the garment cleanly as well. Trim can provide added weight to improve the hang of a garment. It can be serious and refined to add definition or playful and spirited, providing a flicker of movement.

- Zip foot
- Your desired trim

ATTACHING THE TRIM

1. Place the trim and stitch

With wrong sides together, align the long, straight edge of the trim with the raw edge of the garment. Stitch close to the embellished edge of the trim. A zip foot may be helpful. Trim the seam allowance to 6mm (¼").

Trim the garment seam allowance.

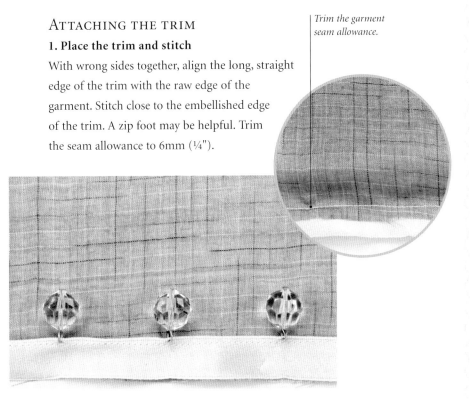

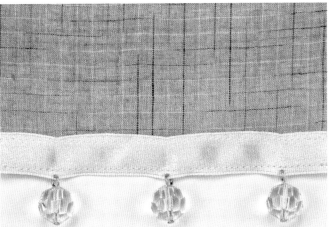

2. Finish stitching the trim

Press the trim to the front of the garment and topstitch the remaining edge of the trim through all thicknesses.

Style suggestion

- This whimsical 'loopy' trim has been stitched to the bottom edge of this skirt in two tiers adding a flicker of movement to the garment.

Flange Closure for Chiffon

The beauty of chiffon is its flowing transparency, a quality which poses challenges in handling and application of construction techniques. This front closure evolved as a method for handling chiffon without adding bulk and tedious hand finishes. The centre front flange, made of silk organza offers enough stability to house machine-worked buttonholes. It also adds to the surface composition and offers an avenue for creativity.

SEWING TOOLS AND MATERIALS

- Silk organza, enough to cut two pieces, each twice the size of the desired flange plus seam allowances

Prepare the pieces

1. Prepare the garment fronts

Cut out garment pieces. Staystitch directly on the centre front seamline of the right and left garment fronts. Follow your pattern directions to make the garment, leaving the centre front edges unfinished but finishing the neckline and hem.

2. Cut the flanges

Measure the length of the centre front and add two seam allowances; this is the length to cut each flange. Decide how wide you want the flange to be and add the width of your seam allowance; double this dimension to find the width to cut the flange. (The finished flange should be at least as wide as the button diameter.) From organza, cut two flanges of the determined dimensions.

3. Sew the flanges

Fold each flange in half lengthways, right sides together. Sew across each end. Trim the seam allowances and turn the flanges right side out; press.

Note
- You can apply the flanges before finishing the neckline and hem but the effect will be nicest if the flange is attached as a final step.

COMPLETE THE CLOSURE

4. Sew on the flanges

With right sides together and raw edges aligned, position a flange on each centre front edge. Sew each in place, stitching directly on top of the staystitching. Stitch again, 6mm (¼") from the raw edge.

5. Press the flanges

Press the work as sewn to embed the stitches. Then fold and press the seam allowances onto the wrong side of the garment so that the flange extends away from the garment.

6. Turn under the raw edges

Turn the garment wrong side up. At each centre front, fold under the raw edge of the seam allowance so that it lies between the flange and garment; press and pin in place.

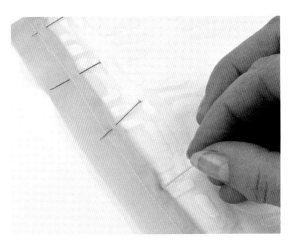

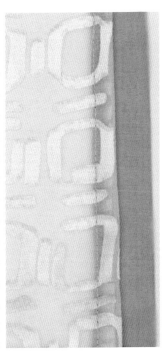

7. Finish the seams

Tack and then topstitch from the right side through all thicknesses.

8. Complete the closure

Work buttonholes in the left front flange. Sew a button to the right front flange opposite each buttonhole.

Style suggestion

• This silk chiffon blouse is finished at centre front with a silk organza flange. This accent produces a clean finish, while also providing a stable housing for buttonholes and buttons.

CHARMEUSE WELT EDGING

The charmeuse welt edging is not only aesthetically pleasing, it performs a valuable service as well; providing an edge finish that enhances the garment without adding bulk. It is important to maintain the fluid drape of soft fabrics, but the edges need a graceful finish. The welt, which is really just a tube, does the job beautifully. The unadulterated welt is a clean, simple tailored finish. The addition of the picot or scallop stitch lends a touch of delicate femininity to the welt. This finish would work well on sheer or lightweight fabrics. They may be crisp or soft and fluid.

SEWING TOOLS AND MATERIALS

- Silk charmeuse, for bias strips for welt
- Hairgrip or tube turner

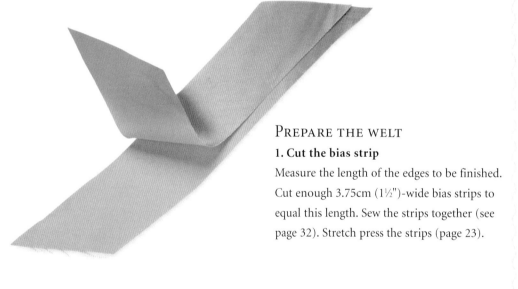

PREPARE THE WELT

1. Cut the bias strip

Measure the length of the edges to be finished. Cut enough 3.75cm (1½")-wide bias strips to equal this length. Sew the strips together (see page 32). Stretch press the strips (page 23).

3. Turn the tube

Cut a small notch in the fold near one end of the tube. Insert a hairgrip through the notch as shown and push it through the tube, which will turn right side out. Try not to rush the turning process or pull the tube with undue force. Gentle encouragement works best.

4. Press the tube

Press the tube flat, positioning the seam at the centre of one side.

2. Fold and sew the strip

Fold the strip in half lengthways, right sides together. Using a small zigzag setting – .5 to .75mm (25 stitches per inch) length and 2 to 2.5mm (10–12 stitches per inch) width – sew 6mm (¼") from the edges to make a tube.

Note

- The small zigzag stitch builds in a bit of stretch, thereby preventing stitches from breaking when the tube is turned right side out.

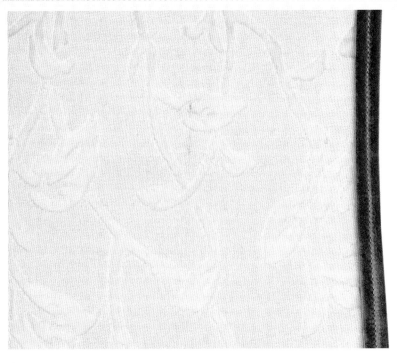

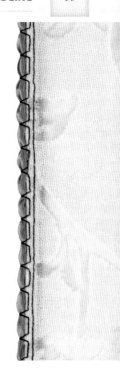

Add a Picot Finish

You may choose to use the blind stitch on the machine to 'picot' or scallop the welt for added verve: position your garment in your machine so that the straight portion of the blind hem stitch falls on the garment and the zigzag stitch crosses and falls off the edge of the welt – it's this single zigzag that pulls the band into a scallop. Test this on a sample to see how it works.

ADD THE WELT TO THE GARMENT EDGE

5. Sew on the welt

Place the edge to be embellished right side up. Position the welt, seam up, aligning the edges. Sew the welt to the garment, stitching 3mm (⅛") from the edge.

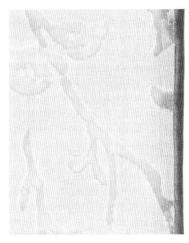

6. Press the edge

With the work wrong side up, using an organza press cloth, fold and press the seam allowances onto the wrong side of garment so that the welt extends away from the garment.

7. Complete the welt edge

With the work right side up, topstitch through all thicknesses close to the seam.

Style suggestion

• This lightweight linen blouse has a charmeuse welt edging encircling the sleeve and collar. The decorative picot stitch was added to the welt for a softer look.

RIBBON-TRIMMED COLLAR BAND

All you need to do to add an artful detail that gives a little surprise to the refined sensibility of a classic band-collar shirt is sew a piece of ribbon to the inside of the band. The ribbon will be visible when the shirt is worn unbuttoned, adding a bit of allure. This is easy to do before you sew the collar and band together.

SEWING TOOLS AND MATERIALS

- Narrow Petersham, satin, or grosgrain ribbon, 6mm to 1.25cm (¼" to ½") wide
- Thin cotton batiste
- A point presser is very helpful

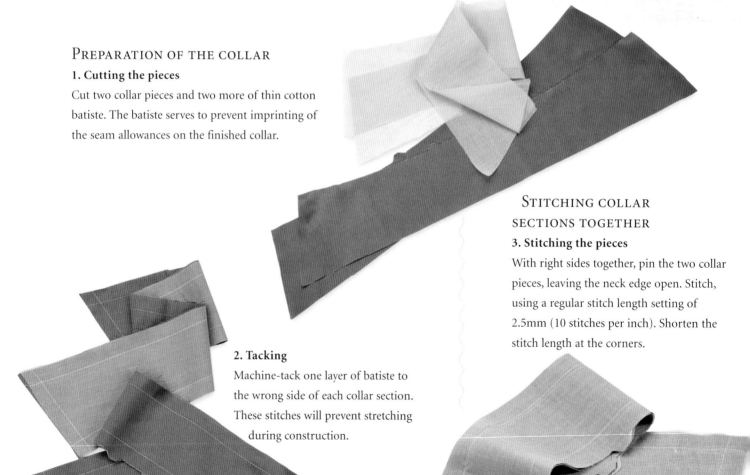

PREPARATION OF THE COLLAR

1. Cutting the pieces

Cut two collar pieces and two more of thin cotton batiste. The batiste serves to prevent imprinting of the seam allowances on the finished collar.

2. Tacking

Machine-tack one layer of batiste to the wrong side of each collar section. These stitches will prevent stretching during construction.

STITCHING COLLAR SECTIONS TOGETHER

3. Stitching the pieces

With right sides together, pin the two collar pieces, leaving the neck edge open. Stitch, using a regular stitch length setting of 2.5mm (10 stitches per inch). Shorten the stitch length at the corners.

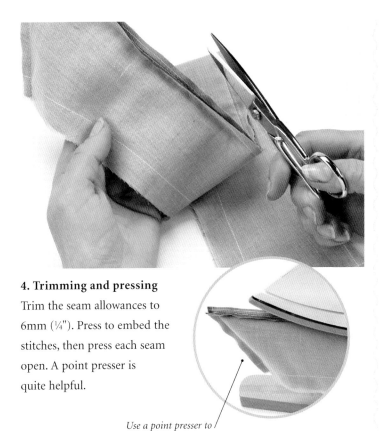

PREPARATION OF THE COLLAR BAND

1. Cutting out

Cut two collar bands and two more of lightweight cotton batiste. The batiste stabilizes the band and enhances the 'stand'. It also helps to support the collar.

4. Trimming and pressing

Trim the seam allowances to 6mm (¼"). Press to embed the stitches, then press each seam open. A point presser is quite helpful.

Use a point presser to press the seams open.

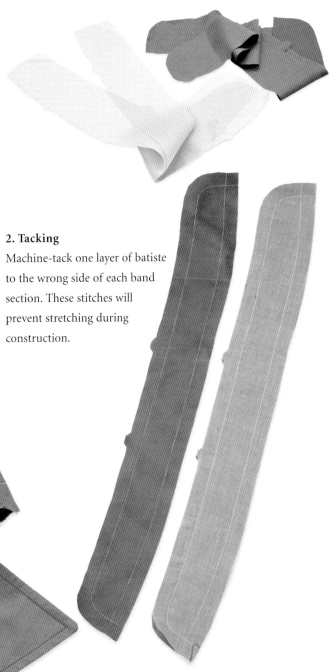

2. Tacking

Machine-tack one layer of batiste to the wrong side of each band section. These stitches will prevent stretching during construction.

FINISHING THE COLLAR

5. Turning right side out

Turn the collar right sides out and press. Tack the raw edges together.

6. Finishing

You may choose to topstitch the finished edges. The collar is now ready to be attached to the collar band.

Embellishing one collar band

3. Cut the ribbon

Cut a length of ribbon long enough to span the collar band and extend into the seam allowance at each end.

4. Sew on the ribbon

Lay the inside collar band right side up. Centre the ribbon on it. Topstitch the ribbon in place along both edges.

5. Attaching the collar to collar band

See Steps 3–6 of Completion of the band, Button-on Garment Sections, pages 80–81 for instructions on joining the collar to the collar band.

Completing the band

6. Pressing and trimming

Turn under the long neck edge of the ribbon-trimmed collar band along the seamline. Press. Trim the seam allowance to 6mm or 1cm (¼" or ⅜").

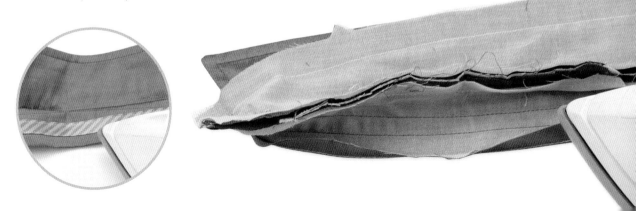

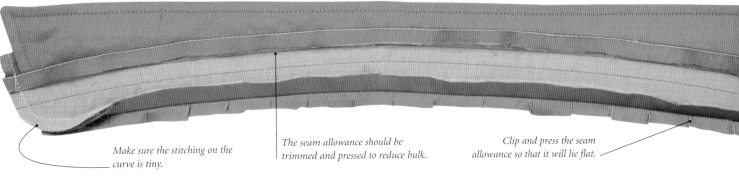

Make sure the stitching on the curve is tiny.

The seam allowance should be trimmed and pressed to reduce bulk.

Clip and press the seam allowance so that it will lie flat.

7. Stitching

With the raw edges even, sandwich the prepared collar between the two collar bands. Pin in place and stitch. Reduce the stitch length as you stitch around the ends of the band.

8. Pressing

Trim seam allowances to 6mm (¼"). You may trim the curved ends of the band slightly smaller. Press to embed the stitches, then press the seam allowances open.

9. Finishing

Turn the collar band right side out and press. The collar and collar band are now ready to attach to the garment.

Style suggestion

- The beauty of this collar is that the ribbon is only seen when the wearer is presenting a more relaxed posture. Subtlety is the focus.

Boned Cuff

This cuff technique is useful when a sharp point or a bold shape is required. It can also be applied to collars. To achieve the effect, a stiff interfacing is used on the inside, without its seam allowances, to support the shape. In order to secure the interfacing a second interlining is needed to hold it in position. The stiff interfacing gives an internal 'skeleton' to support the shape, which would otherwise flop.

SEWING TOOLS AND MATERIALS

- Collar and cuff canvas
- Rigilene boning
- Cotton lawn

Traditional hand-sewn method

1. Cutting the pieces

Create a pattern for the cuff shape with seam allowances added; for each cuff cut out two pieces in fabric. Cut one in cotton lawn and one in stiff interfacing, then remove the seam allowances from the interfacing piece. Cut a strip of boning to provide additional support for the point if necessary.

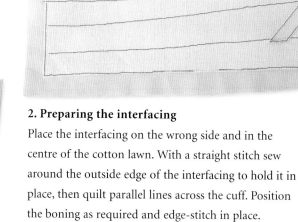

2. Preparing the interfacing

Place the interfacing on the wrong side and in the centre of the cotton lawn. With a straight stitch sew around the outside edge of the interfacing to hold it in place, then quilt parallel lines across the cuff. Position the boning as required and edge-stitch in place.

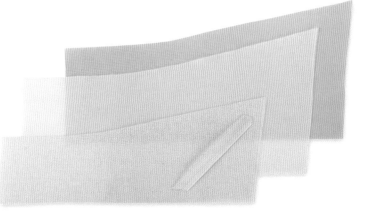

3. Stitching the interfacing to the fabric

Place the cotton lawn on the wrong side of the garment fabric and pin within the seam allowance. Stitch the layers together 3mm (⅛") outside the edge of the stiff interfacing.

4. Managing the seam allowances

Trim the seam allowances to approximately half and press over the interfacing. With a small needle and thread (silk if possible, to prevent tangling) stitch the seam allowances down to the interfacing on all edges except the wrist edge. Mitre the corners and trim more if necessary, to reduce bulk.

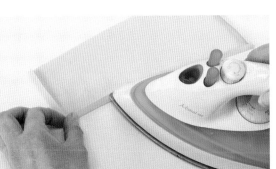

5. Preparing the cuff facing

Take the inside cuff facing and press the seam allowances (except the wrist edge) to the wrong side. Trim excess seam allowance if necessary.

6. Joining the cuff and cuff facing

Place the cuff facing to the wrong side of the cuff, concealing the raw edges inside. Slip-stitch around three edges, leaving the wrist edge free.

Style suggestions

• Use a stiff interfacing within a cuff or collar to hold an intricate shape. Add in the same way as for the boned cuff or use a fine fusible interfacing to sandwich the stiff interfacing in place on the wrong side of the fabric. Trim and snip into the seam allowance before turning through.

The finished cuff; attach it to the sleeve as required.

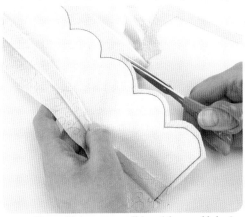

You could shape your cuff; here (above and below), a scalloped pattern is used.

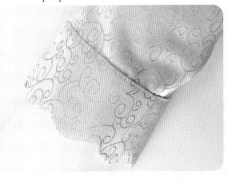

SHOULDER PAD

A shoulder pad should be a discreet padding used to improve and support the shoulder area of a garment. Although in some fashion eras they have been designed to emphasize and enlarge the shoulder silhouette, their primary function is to provide an internal structure or 'skeleton' to ensure that the finished garment holds a perfect shape.

SEWING TOOLS AND MATERIALS

- Foam shoulder pad
- Soft wadding
- Calico/muslin

THE SHOULDER PAD TECHNIQUE

You can use a basic formula to create a shoulder pad to perfectly suit a particular garment and the figure. It should extend from the front notch, up and over the shoulder to the back notches of the armhole and curve smoothly on the inner edge, sitting 3.5cm (1½") from the neck. It can be very thin – suitable for a blouse or dress – or thicker, to take up the space between the shoulder and a tailored jacket or coat. Use more or fewer layers as required and cut appropriately for the garment type.

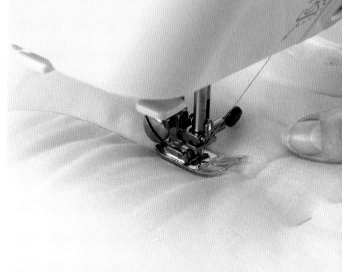

2. Creating the pad

Wrap the outer layers around the pad and pin flat. Sketch the outline shape and size of the required shoulder pad and sew a line of straight stitching to define this line.

1. Collecting the materials required

For one custom shoulder pad, buy a simple, commercially produced pad. Cut a 40cm (16") square of muslin and the same in soft wadding. Place the muslin on the work surface and cover it with the wadding. Fold it diagonally and position the pad in the centre, next to this fold line.

Tip

The muslin layer can be replaced with lining fabric if the shoulder pad will be visible and not concealed under a lining.

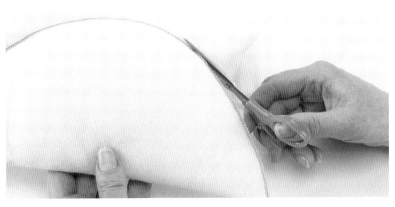

3. Finishing the pad edges

Sew over the line of stitching with a satin stitch (close zigzag), then trim close to the stitches to remove the excess fabric and wadding. Or, use an overlocker for a neat edge.

Above: The finished shoulder pad, seen from inside the jacket. *Below*: The effect on the silhouette of the jacket exterior.

4. Quilting the shoulder pad

Fit a walking foot to the sewing machine for best results; if that is not possible, reduce the pressure of the presser foot – this makes it easier to sew through the thick layers. Lengthen the stitch to 3.5mm (7 stitches per inch). Quilt the layers together, starting across the front edge and spiralling into the centre.

5. Sewing the pad in place

Mould the pad into the shape required and hand-stitch into place at the top of the shoulder. Only sew the centre 10–12cm (4–5") and leave the ends free. Secure the neck edge with a few hand stitches to hold the pad in place.

Style suggestion

• Because it is visible on the inside of the jacket, this shoulder pad is covered in lining fabric to match the jacket lining. Normally shoulder pads are concealed under the lining.

Button-On Garment Sections

Such a fun approach to fashion! This designer technique makes a playful statement, 'now you see it, now you don't'. Separate button-on pieces allow the wearer to derive two or three different looks from one garment. You might experiment with bound buttonholes or tabs (loops) to join the garment sections. The sections themselves may overlap, or, if you use loops, just meet or be slightly separated, depending on the loop length. When you design the pieces, be sure to make the overlapping layer slightly larger than the piece it covers, so that the two fit smoothly together when the garment wraps around your body. The exact amount of the adjustment will vary, depending on the style of the garment and thickness of the fabric, so plan to test.

- Lightweight cotton batiste
- Buttons

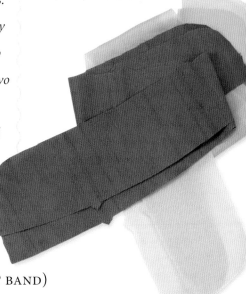

Make a detachable collar

Prepare the collar following the steps on pages 70 and 71. This designer technique will have two collar bands. The first one will be attached to the garment and the second will accompany the detachable collar.

Band one (garment band)

1. Cutting out

Cut two collar bands and two more of lightweight cotton batiste. The batiste stabilizes the band and helps support the buttons and the detachable collar.

2. Tacking

Machine-tack one layer of batiste to the wrong side of each band section. These stitches will prevent stretching during construction.

COMPLETION OF THE BAND

3. Pressing and trimming

Turn under the long neck edge of one band section along the seamline. Press. Trim the seam allowance to 1cm (⅜").

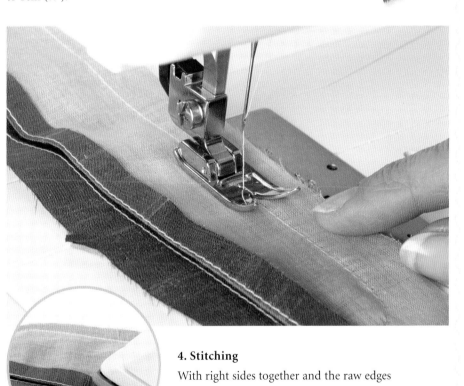

4. Stitching

With right sides together and the raw edges even, pin the band sections. Stitch, leaving the neck edge open. Reduce the stitch length as you stitch the ends of the band.

5. Pressing

Trim the seam allowances to 6mm (¼"). You may trim the curved ends of the band slightly smaller. Press to embed the stitches, then press the seam allowances open. Turn the collar band right side out and press. The collar band is now ready to attach to the garment.

6. Adding buttons

After attaching the band to the garment, edge-stitch all around the band. Sew buttons (the size and number are optional) to the collar band. The button placement should be compatible with the buttonholes on the detachable collar. They will serve as embellishment when the detachable collar is not being worn.

Band two (collar band)

1. Cutting out

Cut two collar bands and two more of lightweight cotton batiste. The batiste stabilizes the band and helps to support the buttonholes and the collar.

Patternwork for detachable collar

Lengthen the collar band for the detachable collar by 6mm (¼"). Do this by slashing the pattern at the shoulder markings and spreading 3mm (⅛") at each shoulder. This band needs to be slightly longer because it functions as an outer layer.

2. Tacking

Machine-tack one layer of batiste to the wrong side of each band section. These stitches will prevent stretching during construction.

Completion of the band

3. Pressing and trimming

Turn under the long neck edge of both band sections along the seamline. Press. Trim the seam allowance to 1cm (⅜").

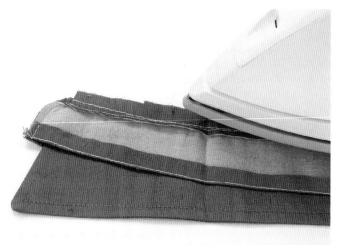

4. Pinning and stitching

With the raw edges even, sandwich the prepared collar between the two bands. Pin in place and stitch. Reduce the stitch length as you stitch around the ends of the band.

5. Trimming and pressing

Trim seam allowances to 6mm (¼"). You may trim the curved ends of the band slightly smaller. Press to embed the stitches, then press the seam allowances open.

6. Finishing

Turn the collar band right side out and press. Hand-tack the bottom edges together. Edge-stitch all the way around the collar band.

7. Making buttonholes

Make machine-worked buttonholes in the collar band.

When you make the cuffs, sew loops into the top seam. Sew buttons around each sleeve, spacing them to correspond to the loops, at a level that places the cuff where you wish relative to the wrist.

Style suggestions

Detachable collar

- The shirt may be worn with the collar band alone, which would showcase the buttons. The addition of the collar completely removes the buttons from view and entirely changes the look and feel of the shirt.

Detachable cuffs

- This silk jacket can be worn without the contrasting detachable cuffs, and could be layered over a slim-fitting long-sleeve tee for a more casual look. When the jacket is worn without the cuffs, the buttons become 'baubles' or accents, adding a decorative accent of their own. The cuff may be added for a more polished, dressier presentation.

CHAPTER THREE

DESIGN DETAILS: CONCEALED

The following pages will introduce the enthusiastic seamster to a myriad of hidden treasures and secrets that enhance the wearer's experience. Not everything needs to be seen by the public at large. The luxurious sensation of sliding a hand into a satin pocket, or the convenience of a 'flip-out' pouch are just two of the delicious details offered in this chapter.

Concealed foundations

The crispness of a couture garment
relies on the structure of inventive
hidden foundations.
*Zang Toi Autumn 2006 Show, Olympus
Fashion Week, New York*

LINING/BINDING SKIRT PANELS

This lining/binding technique works well on fairly straight seams with minimal curves. It is suitable for panel skirts, trousers and unstructured rectangular-shaped jackets. It gives a beautiful, clean and efficient finish. It results in the garment being lined and seams finished with minimal effort.

- Lining fabric

THE LINING/BINDING TECHNIQUE

1. Cutting out

Cut the pieces of the garment according to the pattern. Cut the lining seams to be bound 1.5cm (⅝") wider than the pattern.

2. Sewing the seams

With right sides together and raw edges aligned, sew 6mm (¼") seams to be bound.

3. Pressing and stitching

Press to embed the stitches. Press the seams away from the garment. Turn the garment section right side out and press again. Stitch the top edges together.

4. Stitching

You may choose to stitch-in-the-ditch (see Glossary, page 156) if you are working with a slippery lining.

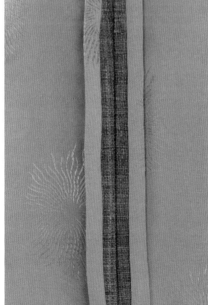

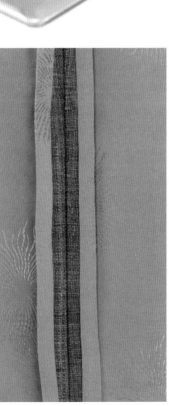

5. Finishing

Sew the garment sections together as usual. Press to embed the stitches. Press the seams open.

Style suggestions

Top: The lining/binding
- This technique results in an attractively finished lining and seams for relatively little effort.

Bottom: Reinforcing the slit
- This subtle, age-old designer trick provides maximum benefit from minimal labour. The 'bar' from a hook-and-eye set is placed strategically at the top of the skirt slit to reduce the chances of the seam coming undone under stress.

COUTURE WAISTBAND

The couture method of constructing a waistband results in a superior product. The band does not roll, yet it is comfortable, and lies flat. There is no extra bulk so it is particularly compatible with thicker woollens where a double layer of face fabric would simply not work. This technique is time-consuming but worth all the effort.

SEWING TOOLS AND MATERIALS

- Silk organza
- Tailor's canvas or other stiff interfacing
- Petersham ribbon

THE COUTURE WAISTBAND TECHNIQUE

1. Cutting out
Cut a waistband to the finished length and width you need, plus seam allowances. Cut one in fabric and one in silk organza. Then cut a third band in tailor's canvas, and remove the seam allowances.

2. Stitching the seams
Mark the seamlines on the organza. Place the tailor's canvas between the seamlines. Channel stitch the canvas to the organza. Aim for 3mm (⅛") spacing in order to add stability without bulk. Press.

3. Tacking
Place the stabilized organza on the wrong side of the waistband, and machine-tack in place. Press.

4. Stitching Petersham

Cut a strip of Petersham ribbon the length of the waistband. It should be 6mm (¼") wider than the finished band. Working on the right side of the waistband, place one long edge of the Petersham along the fold line of the band. Make sure it is a scant 3mm (⅛") away from the fold line so it will not show when the garment is completed. Stitch it in place. Press to embed the stitches. Press the band along the fold line.

Style suggestions

- This construction method results in a beautiful, stable waistband that conforms to the figure without adding bulk.

5. Stitching and pressing

With the right sides together, pin the waistband to the garment. Stitch, trim and press.

6. Finishing

On the reverse side of the garment, sew the Petersham ribbon down by hand.

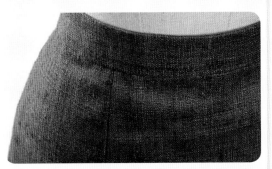

High-Waist Couture Facing

This couture approach to constructing a waist facing works well on any waistline where a waistband is not desired. It is particularly well suited to trousers and skirts with high waists. The channel stitching and the bones add structure and support while maintaining a clean line.

- Silk organza
- Tailor's canvas
- Rigilene boning

The couture facing technique

1. Taping the waistline

Prepare the garment as usual so it is ready for the facing. Now tape the waistline to prevent stretching during wear. This basic step is extremely important for all faced waistlines. Place stay tape over the seamline and stitch it in place.

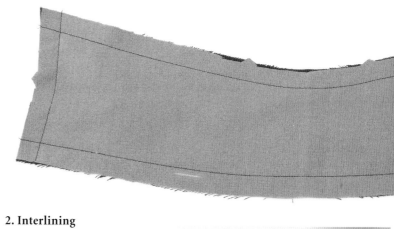

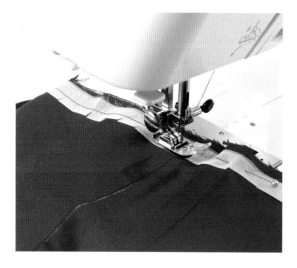

2. Interlining

Interline the facing with silk organza and mark the stitching lines.

3. Channel stitching

Remove the seam allowances from the interfacing and position it on the organza side of the facing, between the marked seamlines. Channel stitch through all thicknesses using 6mm (¼") spacing. A walking foot may be helpful.

Note
- This technique is most efficient when the facing extends 1.2cm (½") below the natural waistline.

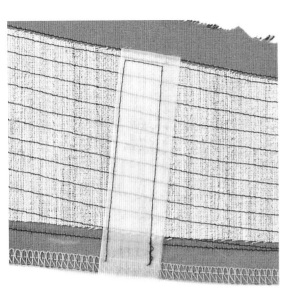

4. Adding boning channels

Add boning channels where required. The important locations include seams and the areas of the facing that correspond to dart placement on the garment. The channels should stop a generous 3mm (⅛") short of any seamlines. Stitch through all the thicknesses, leaving the bottom end open.

5. Adding bones

Insert bones into the boning channels. Stitch the lower ends of the boning channels, encasing the bones. It is wise to singe the ends of the bones so that they are less inclined to poke through.

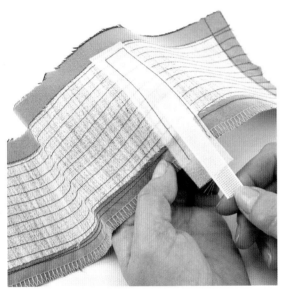

6. Finishing

Trim away the excess channel, and finish the edge of the facing.

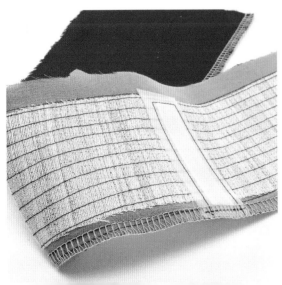

Note

- To make boning channels, cut a long, 5cm (2") wide strip of silk organza on the lengthways grain and fold it in half lengthways. Press. Cut into the lengths you need.

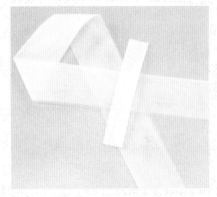

Silk organza and boning.

Style suggestion

- The high-waist couture facing may be used effectively on both trousers and skirts.

EASY TWIN-NEEDLE HEM

Here is a wonderfully easy way to make a beautiful, flat hem: back the entire hem with a fusible interfacing, and topstitch with a twin needle. The resulting hem gives your garment a sporty, energetic look – with no rippling. This technique is especially good for knit or woven fabrics with a bit of Lycra introduced to provide some stretch. If the hem needs to stretch in order for the garment to fit over your head or hips, choose a stretch interfacing.

- Fusible lightweight interfacing
- Twin needle

PREPARE THE HEM

1. Determine the garment length

It is much easier to do this step before garment pieces are assembled, so determine the length and cut the hem allowance to the required depth.

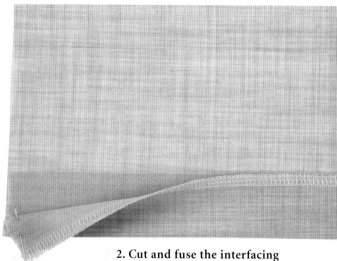

2. Cut and fuse the interfacing

For each piece to be hemmed, cut a strip of fusible interfacing twice the depth of the finished hem. Place each garment piece wrong side up, lay the corresponding strip of interfacing on it, aligning with the bottom edge, and fuse in place.

3. Construct the garment

Referring to your pattern directions, sew your garment together, ready to hem.

FINISH THE HEM

4. Press the hem fold

With the garment wrong side up, fold up
the lower edge so it is even with the top
edge of the fusible interfacing and press the
hem fold. (No more measuring when the
garment is in the round – it has already been
done when you cut the interfacing to twice
the hem depth!)

*There is a neat zigzag of
stitching on the reverse
of the garment.*

5. Sew the hem

Install the twin needle in your machine. From
the right side, topstitch the hem in place.
(Place a piece of masking tape on your
machine bed as a guide if the hem is deep.)

Note
• If you wish, overlock the raw edge
  for a cleaner look.

Style suggestions
• The twin-needle hem is a real time-saver
  that produces professional results. It is a
  clean and durable finish that can also be
  used on armholes and necklines.

Organza 'Bubble' Hem Finish

To prevent the lower edge of a sheath dress or skirt from collapsing close to the legs and inhibiting movement, slip a folded bias band of organza between the hem allowance and garment body. You don't press the fold of this band, so it makes a bubble-like spacer inside the hem. This clever, innovative and very simple technique proves once again that versatile organza is an item of high standing in the well-stocked sewing armoury.

- Silk organza, enough to cut a bias strip 12.5cm (5") wide and the length of the garment hemline circumference

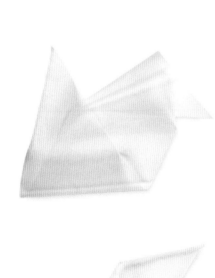

Prepare the organza bubble

1. Cut the bias strip

Cut a 12.5cm (5")-wide bias strip of silk organza the length of the hemline plus extra for overlap. In this instance you may piece the strip because it is hidden from view and will not affect the function.

2. Fold and stitch the bias strip

Fold the organza strip in half lengthways. Do not press it – you want the fold to stay soft. Staystitch the raw edges together using a 1.25cm (½") seam allowance. Do not stretch-press before you fold, the curve of the organza helps the bubble to do its work.

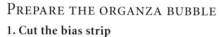

Hem the garment

3. Prepare the hem

Mark, fold and press the hem at the bottom of your garment; finish the top edge of the hem allowance as you wish. A 6.5cm (2½") hem depth is ideal. Lay the garment wrong side up and unfold the hem.

The organza attached to the hem, seen from the right side.

Seen from the reverse side, the skirt hem is unfolded and the organza is attached to the lining.

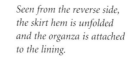

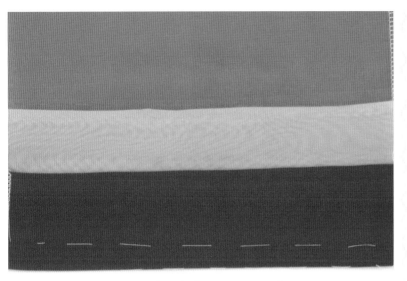

4. Attach the organza to the garment

Orientating the raw edges towards the hem fold, lay the organza strip on the hem allowance, overlapping by 2cm (¾"). If the bottom of the garment is a tube, lap the ends of the strip one over the other; do not join with a seam. Sew the organza to the hem allowance by machine, stitching along the staystitching.

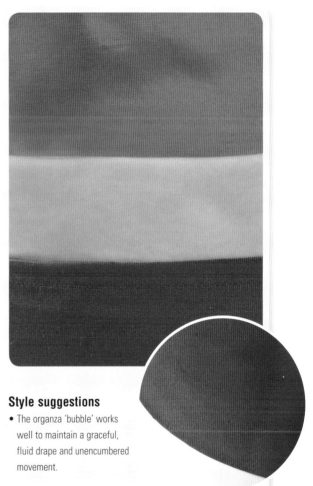

Style suggestions
- The organza 'bubble' works well to maintain a graceful, fluid drape and unencumbered movement.

The organza 'bubble' hem viewed from the right side.

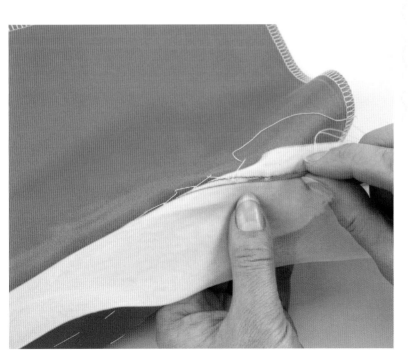

5. Sew the hem

Fold the hem allowance into place again. Sew the hem by hand, using a catch stitch or other hand stitch of your choice and placing the stitches through the hem allowance along the seam of the organza – so that the folded edge of the organza remains loose.

FACED HEM

A faced hem is the perfect way to finish a skirt where a deep hem is required on a shaped or curved edge. A typical example would be on a wedding gown with a train, where the shape of the hem would make a deep hem difficult to produce neatly though it would give the necessary weight in order for the skirt to drape well. The hem is created by cutting facing pieces from the skirt pattern, the same shape as the lower edge. These pieces are sewn to the lower edge and pressed to the wrong side, where they fit perfectly.

SEWING TOOLS AND MATERIALS

- Dress netting
- Pattern paper

Tip

If the honeycomb structure of the netting shows through the fabric, sandwich a second layer of suitable interlining (for example, cotton lawn) between the fabric and the net.

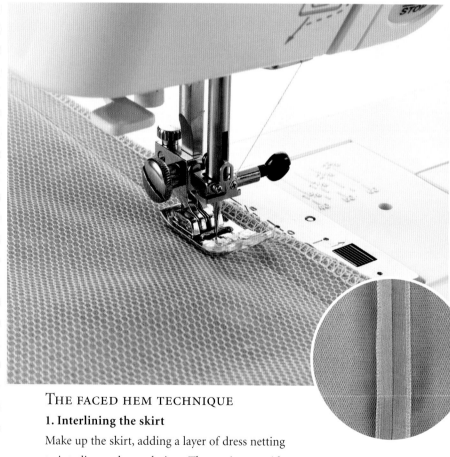

THE FACED HEM TECHNIQUE

1. Interlining the skirt

Make up the skirt, adding a layer of dress netting to interline each panel piece. The netting provides the 'skeleton' for you to attach the hem stitches to and also provides support for the skirt.

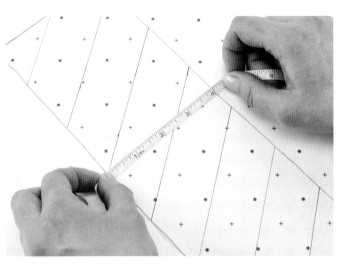

2. Making the facing pattern

Draw a line 10cm (4") above the lower edge of the pattern pieces. Trace these onto pattern paper and cut out the facings for the hem.

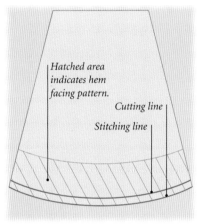

Hatched area indicates hem facing pattern.

Cutting line

Stitching line

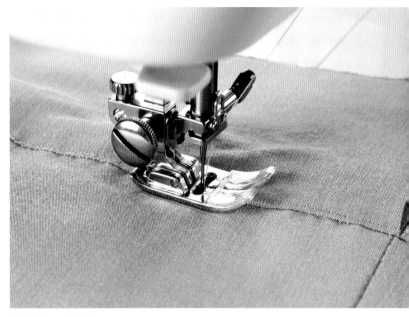

4. Understitching

Press the seam flat first to set the stitches, then press the seam allowances and facing together away from the skirt. Understitch through these layers, close to the seam, to hold them together. This will keep the facing from rolling towards the right side of the skirt.

3. Stitching

Match each facing piece to the hem edge, with right sides placed together, and pin. Fold the seam allowances in where the pieces join so that there'll be a neat finish on the reverse of the garment. Stitch 1.5cm (⅝") above the cut edge all around the hem.

5. Finishing

Fold the facing to the wrong side and tuck the top edge down 12mm (½"). Slip-stitch the facings together at the seams and slip-stitch the folded hem to the dress net. Do not stitch through to the fabric or the stitches will be seen from the right side.

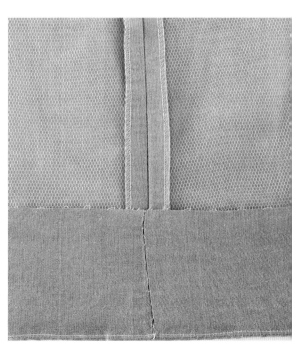

HORSEHAIR BRAID HEM

To support a hem and give it more rigidity, you can sew horsehair braid (or 'crin trim') to the hem. Generally it is sewn into the lining or petticoat of a skirt, but it can be stitched to the fabric itself. Horsehair braid is made from bias-woven nylon and is available in wide and narrow widths. It supports the hem without adding bulk and keeps it from collapsing, giving a much softer effect than hooping a skirt with wire. There are various ways to apply horsehair braid. The two described here give neat finishes and are easy to sew.

SEWING TOOLS AND MATERIALS

- Horsehair braid

SEWING HORSEHAIR BRAID INTO A FACED HEM

1. Preparing the faced hem

Prepare the skirt, and pin and sew the facing pieces to the lower edges of the hem. Before edge-stitching or pressing to the wrong side, go to Step 2.

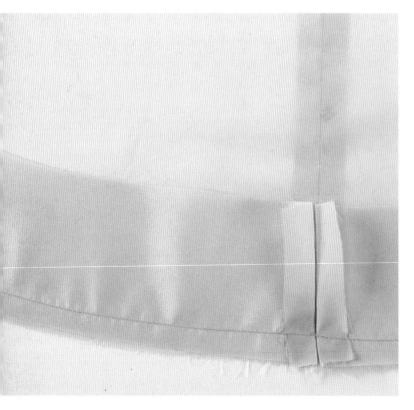

2. Applying horsehair braid to the seam allowances

With the wrong side of the skirt uppermost and the facings hidden below, pin the horsehair braid to the seam allowances; the edge of the braid should lie next to the stitching. Stitch close to the edge, sewing through the horsehair braid and the seam allowances, taking care not to stretch the braid in the process. At the end, overlap the horsehair braid and cut off the excess.

3. Pressing the facing to the inside

Fold the facing up into place on the inside of the skirt, enclosing the horsehair braid in the process. Press lightly with the seam and the understitching on the inside, leaving a smooth finish on the right side.

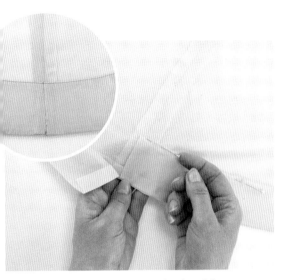

4 Enclosing the horsehair in the faced hem

Slip-stitch the facings at the seams and tuck under a seam allowance on the upper facing edge. Pin and sew the hem facing in place, leaving the upper edge of the braid free. If the horsehair braid is being applied to a lining, machine edge-stitch it into position. If the braid is being sewn directly to the hem of a skirt or dress, hand-stitch it neatly to the interlining.

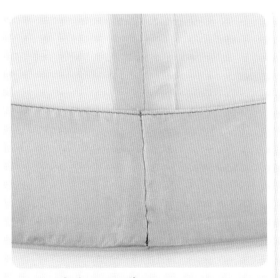

Style suggestion
- The horsehair braid hem is easy to apply and gives the hem a crisp finish.

Concealing Horsehair Braid in the Hem

The nylon threads of the horsehair braid have a rough texture that could snag tights. For this reason it is best to ensure that it is wrapped fully and not just sewn to the inside edge of the hem.

1. Marking the skirt length

Check the length required for the finished garment and mark this with tacking or a chalk line on the wrong side of the fabric. Place the horsehair braid below the marked hemline and measure 6mm (¼") from the horsehair braid. Trim the entire hem to this newly marked length.

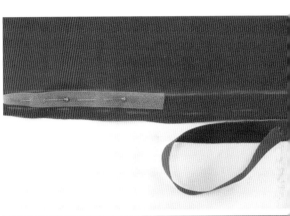

2. Sewing the horsehair braid

On the wrong side of the fabric, overlap the horsehair braid over the lower 6mm (¼") of the hem. Pin and machine-stitch the braid to the hem edge, taking care not to stretch the horsehair braid in the process. Overlap the ends and snip away the excess.

3. Folding up the hem

Fold the braid to the wrong side of the skirt hem, then fold again to hide the braid and raw edge within the hem. Secure the hem with machine topstitching or with hand slip-stitches as appropriate.

BALANCED DART

Seams and darts are used in garment making to give shape and to achieve a good fit. In the case of a conventional dart, the fabric is folded and sewn to remove fullness and pressed to one side. However, this leaves bulk on one side of the dart and, effectively, a seam sitting along one edge. By balancing the dart with extra fabric a flatter, smoother finish can be achieved, even though fabric has been added.

- Spare pieces of the garment fabric

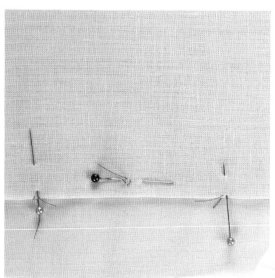

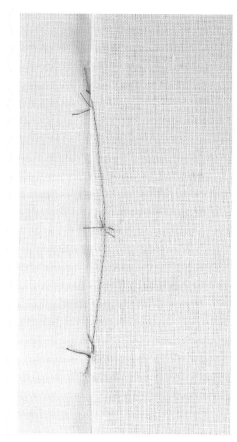

THE BALANCED DART TECHNIQUE

1. Transferring pattern markings

Transfer the markings from the pattern using tailor's tacks, and fold the dart through the centre with right sides together – matching up the tailor's tacks. Pin the dart into position for sewing.

2. Cutting extra fabric

Cut a rectangle of the garment fabric, longer and wider than the dart. Place this under the dart and re-pin to hold all the layers together.

3. Sewing the dart

Start at one end of the dart in the excess cloth and stitch onto the point of the dart along the sewing line and off at the other end onto the excess fabric below.

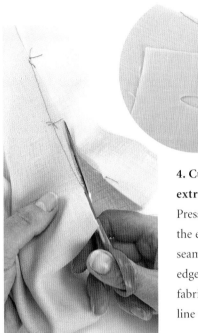

4. Cutting away the extra fabric

Press the dart flat, then pull the extra fabric away from the seamline towards the folded edge. Cut away the excess fabric (not the garment!) in line with the folded edge.

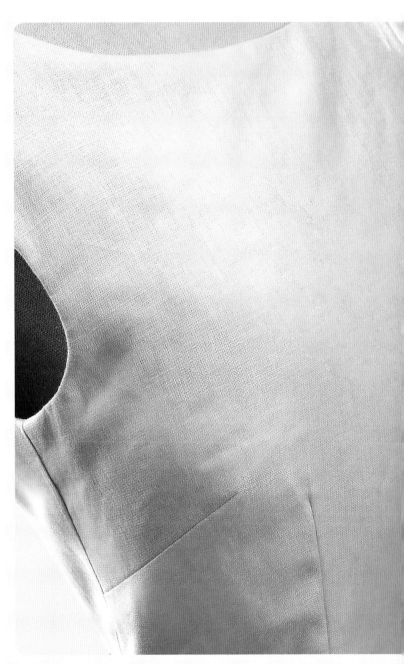

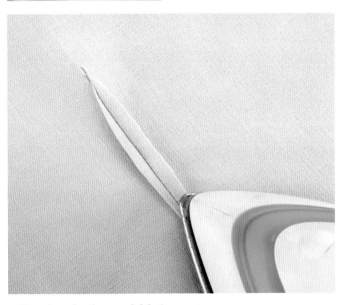

5. Pressing the dart and fabric apart

Press the dart one way and the extra fabric the other way using the point of the iron. Turn over and lightly press the surface of the garment using a press cloth to protect the fabric. You will achieve a beautiful smooth shape.

Style suggestion

• Use this technique on all weights of fabric from fine silks to thicker linens and wools. It works well for dresses and skirts.

COUTURE DART

The 'couture dart' is a wonderful method for sewing a dart that has been passed down through the generations. Surprisingly, it is not widely known, though it should be. This dart works well on all fabrics, and it is essential when working with sheers. There are no unsightly thread ends at the tip of the dart… just a clean, graceful finish.

- Needle threader

THE COUTURE DART TECHNIQUE

1. Marking the dart

Mark the dart on the wrong side of the fabric.

2. Threading the machine

Next, thread the machine needle. Pull the bobbin thread through the needle from back to front. Tie the top thread to the bobbin thread so there is one continuous thread. Then wind the thread back so that the knot won't get caught in the thread tension.

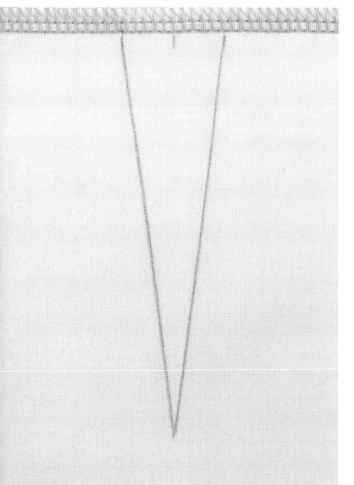

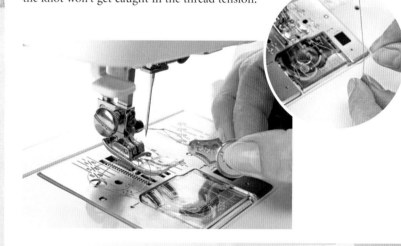

3. Sewing the dart

Start sewing the dart at its tip; do not backstitch. Once you have finished sewing each dart, you will have to rethread the needle for the next.

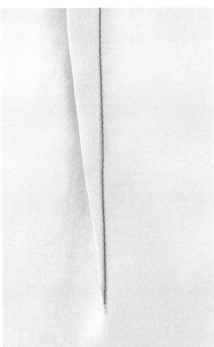

The finished dart.

Style suggestions

- **Left**: Two examples of the dart worked on thicker, woollen fabrics. There are no puckers at the tip, just a beautiful, flat finish with no added bulk.
- **Right**: Two examples of the dart worked on sheer fabrics. Top, used as a dart, and bottom, an example of tucks on a sheer fabric using the couture dart technique. Each tuck is stitched beginning at the tip.

SATIN POCKET BAGS

Some designer techniques are implemented purely for the enjoyment of the person wearing the garment. In elevating a garment to couture status, there often are many unsung, unseen heroes. The satin pocket bag is one of these elements; a luxurious detail, not meant to be seen by the casual observer but sure to enhance the mood of the wearer. How nice it will be when the sumptuous feel of satin greets your fingers when you slip your hand into your pocket. This technique is explained for a front waist pocket on trousers, but you could adapt it for any pocket that requires a separate bag.

- Scrap of silk organza
- Satin, small amount for pocket bag

PREPARE THE PIECES

1. Draft the pattern

Determine the size and shape of the pocket opening. You should be able to slide your hand into the pocket with ease. A 15cm (6") opening is standard for a waist pocket. You should not need to adapt the commercial pattern if you are using one, other than to use satin for the pocket bags.

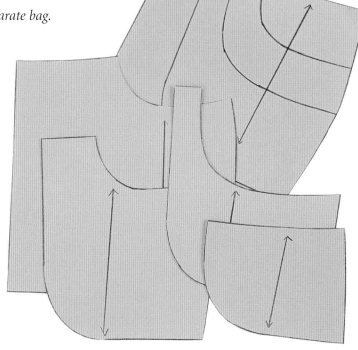

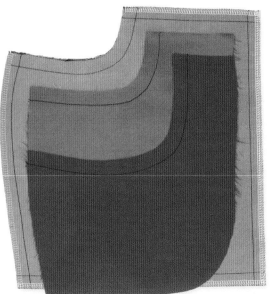

2. Cut the pieces

Cut the trouser front and side front from your fashion fabric. Cut the front facing/bag and the trouser side-front bag from the satin.

Notes

- It seems that most ready-to-wear is outfitted with short pocket bags, which are not safe to hold valuables. You may make your bags as deep as you like.

- Satins come in different weights. If you want a more durable bag use a heavier satin.

- The point for adding a pocket during the trouser construction may vary depending on your pattern or your preference. Incorporate this method at the appropriate time for the garment you are making.

STABILIZE THE OPENING

3. Tape the opening with silk organza

Cut a straight-grain strip of silk organza about 3cm (1¼") wide and as long as the pocket opening. Press it in half lengthways. Lay the trouser front wrong side up; centre the organza strip directly over the seamline on the pocket opening. Stitch in place, clipping the organza as needed around

4. Staystitch the pieces

Staystitch the pocket opening edge of the trouser front facing and side-front bag. Also staystitch the waist seamline of the trouser front and trouser side front.

SEW THE FACING/BAG TO THE TROUSER FRONT

5. Attach the pieces

Place the trouser front and facing/bag right sides together, with the raw edges of the pocket opening aligned. Sew them together. Trim and clip the seam allowances. Press the seam open.

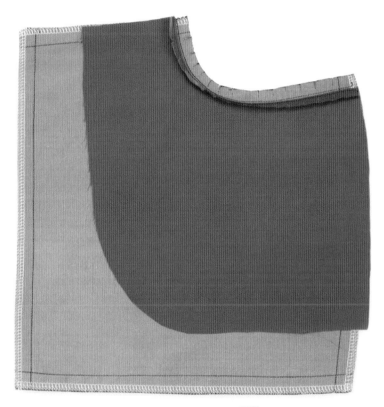

6. Turn and stitch the edge

Turn the facing/bag to the inside of the trouser front along the seam. Press the seamed edge. From right side, topstitch through all thicknesses close to the edge.

SEW THE SIDE-FRONT BAG TO THE SIDE FRONT

7. Attach the pieces

On the inside curved edge of the side-front bag, clip the seam allowance up to the staystitching. Then, with right sides together and raw edges aligned, pin and sew the inside curve of the bag to the bottom (outside curve) of the side front.

8. Unfold and stitch the edge

Unfold the pieces so that they lie flat and the bag extends from the side front. Press the seam allowance towards the bag. Overlock-finish the raw edges of the seam allowance together if you wish. From right side, topstitch through all thicknesses close to the seam.

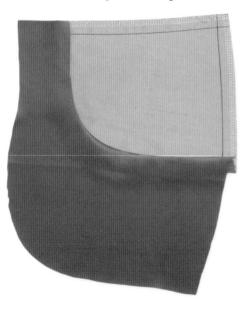

COMPLETE THE POCKET

9. Align the side front and front

Lay the side front right side up. Position the trouser front right side up on top of it, aligning the waist and side edges. Pin together along the pocket opening.

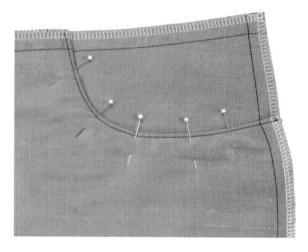

10. Sew the bag pieces together

Turn the work over. Smooth the bag layers to be sure they are flat; pin together along the outside edges (leave free from the trouser front). Sew the pocket bag layers together along their outside edge from the waist, along the bottom, and up the side to wherever they intersect with the side seam on the trouser side-front. Overlock-finish the edge of the seam allowance if you wish.

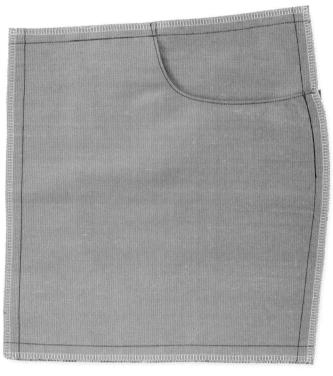

11. Sew the front to the side front

Press the seam just sewn. Lay the trousers right side up; tack the front to the side front where they overlap at the waist and side seam. Remove the pins from the pocket opening.

Note
- On some patterns, the pocket bag is shaped to be sewn into the side seam, not to hang loose as shown. Refer to your pattern directions to complete steps 10 and 11.

Waistline 'Flip Out' Pouch

Here is a little zipped hanging pocket to add to the inside of a pair of trousers or a skirt to provide secure hidden storage for a credit card, change or lipstick. It's a very practical solution for travellers or just for those times when carrying a handbag is not optimal. When you need whatever it carries, slip your hand inside the waist of your garment and pull the pocket up and out.

SEWING TOOLS AND MATERIALS

- Cards or other paper for template
- Lightweight, firmly woven fabric, small amount for pocket
- Lightweight zip, 5" (12.5cm) long
- Double-fold bias tape or 1.25cm (½")-wide Petersham ribbon, piece 61cm (24") long

PREPARE THE PIECES

1. Draft the pattern.

To make a template for the pocket, draft a 8.5cm x 12.5cm (3½" x 5") rectangle and round two corners on one longer edge as shown. Cut it out.

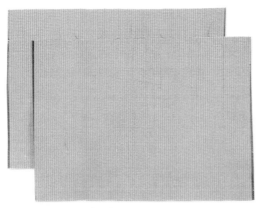

2. Cut the fabric

Cut two pieces of fabric, each 17cm x 12.5cm (7" x 5").

3. Prepare the rectangles

Fold each rectangle in half widthways, right side out; press the fold. On each, using the template as a guide, round the corners on the edge opposite the fold; then tack the raw edges together a short distance from edge.

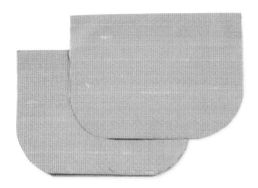

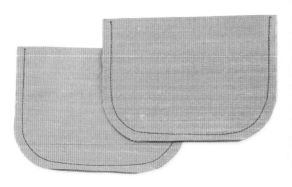

MAKE THE POCKET

4. Install the zip

Position the bag pieces on your table side-by-side with the folded edges meeting. Pin the zip between them, making sure the top and bottom stops are inset from the ends by at least 1cm (⅜"). Sew the zip in place.

5. Close the pouch

Fold the two halves of the pocket together along the zip (zip tape should be inside, between them) and tack the raw edges together over the previous stitching.

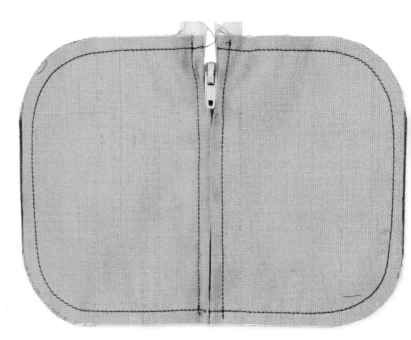

Note

• If using Petersham ribbon, press it in half lengthways. Then dip it in water, lay it on your ironing board, and curve it to the shape of the pocket, and then press dry with your iron.

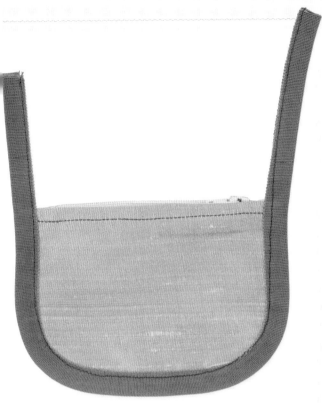

6. Bind the edge

Centre the bias binding or Petersham (see note) on the edge opposite the zip. Then slide the binding over the edge so it is encased, pinning it in place. Topstitch the open edge of the binding from one end to the other, securing it to the pocket.

7. Attach the pocket to your garment

Sew the ends of the binding into the waist seam of your garment. The ideal placement is about 8cm (3½") towards the side from centre front, with the top hanging about 7.5cm (3") below the waistband. Our bodies have a hollow space there that easily conceals the bag.

Style suggestion

• The flip-out pouch is great for the traveller who doesn't want to carry a bag. It is the perfect size for necessities. Women also find it useful for inter-office meetings and appointments.

CHAPTER FOUR

DESIGNER UNDERPINNINGS

This chapter of the book is a 'behind the scenes' approach to fashion. Fashion fabrics all have their own distinct, unique qualities and characteristics; their individual personalities. You will select fabrics depending on your intentions for a particular garment, but you can manipulate how a fabric behaves by teaming it with a 'companion fabric' or 'underpinning'.

Ensemble piece

Hard-working members of the ensemble of fabrics used in a couture garment contribute to the support of the design while remaining behind the scenes.

John Galliano for Christian Dior Haute Couture show, Spring/Summer 2009, Paris Fashion Week

INTERLINING LUXURY FABRICS

The characteristics of a luxury fabric may be enhanced or inhibited by backing or interlining them with various companion fabrics. See the Directory of Luxury Fabrics *for more information on fabric, page 116.*

If you wanted to make a structured, form-fitting jacket out of silk velvet, an interlining would be required to facilitate that process. Silk velvet is naturally fluid and drapey, so adding a structural interlining would allow you to mould the fabric to the figure.

Use of companion fabric backings does broaden the versatility of the fashion fabric. This chapter shows you how to use silk dupioni, silk velvet, lightweight wool and silk charmeuse as companion fabrics.

Treatment of the Fabrics

The backing technique is the same for all of the samples (see page 145). Be sure to pre-treat all interlinings/backings in the same manner as the fashion fabric. If the garment is to be laundered, pre-launder the fashion fabric and the interlining. If dry-cleaning is in order, do the same for the fabric and its companion. There is nothing worse than having an interlining shrink after a garment has been completed.

Prepare each garment piece to be backed before any construction takes place. Cut both the garment fabric and the companion fabric in the same way, and hand-tack them together in the seam allowances. You can now treat each garment section as one piece.

Using more than one companion

One garment may utilize several different fabrics for various effects. For example, a dupioni gown may have hair canvas backing a floor-length A-line or princess-line skirt for extra 'stand-out' power, while the shawl collar and turned back cuffs may be interlined with flannel for loft and softness. The bodice of the same gown may be backed with batiste to facilitate shaping the design to the figure.

Choices of companion fabrics are endless. Feel free to experiment. It is always wise to check the compatibility of the two fabrics before cutting out an entire garment. Make small samples to determine what works best.

Silk Dupioni Backed with Flannel

This silk dupioni skirt is half-backed with cotton flannel (on the left), and the other half is not backed with anything. Notice the dramatic difference in appearance – you can see that the flannel adds weight and depth to the dupioni. The overall appearance is softer and more sumptuous, while also encouraging the skirt to hang slightly away from the body. The unbacked skirt looks limp and tired by comparison.

Backing silk dupioni

Unbacked dupioni would be preferable in a fitted, tailored shirt. Any backing would detract from that particular fashion statement. Look at the dupioni shirt on page 73 (Ribbon-Trimmed Collar Band). The crisp quality of the fabric works well in this application. The silk dupioni sheath dress on page 53 (Channel-Stitched Accents) was interlined with cotton batiste to assist in moulding the dupioni to the figure and to receive the added stress in the hip area. The bodice and hem were backed with cotton flannel.

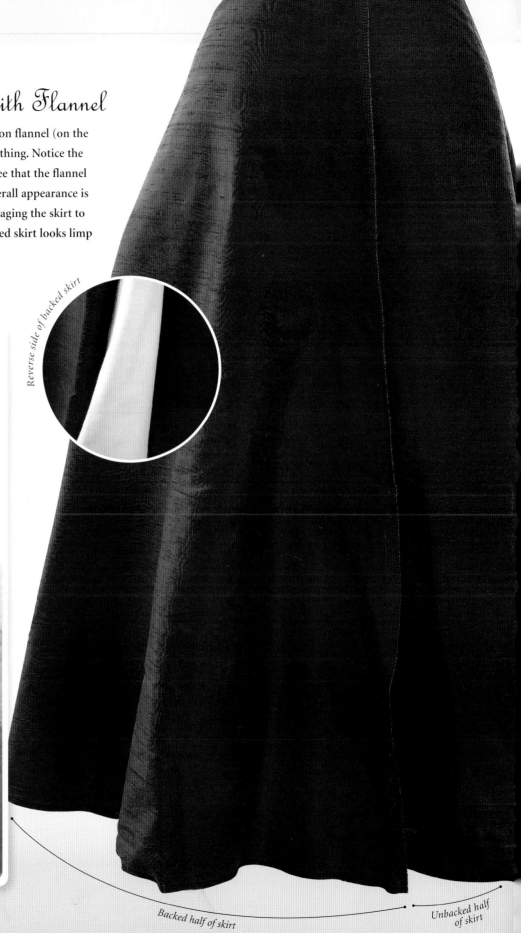

Reverse side of backed skirt

Backed half of skirt

Unbacked half of skirt

Lightweight Wool

Lightweight wool has a nice drape, although it is a bit sheer for daylight and would require a slip. This is one function of an interlining – eliminating the need for added intimate apparel. In the examples below, the right-hand sides of the skirts are left unbacked for contrast.

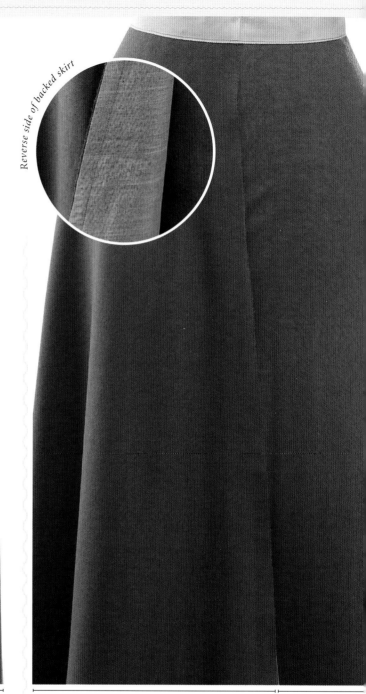

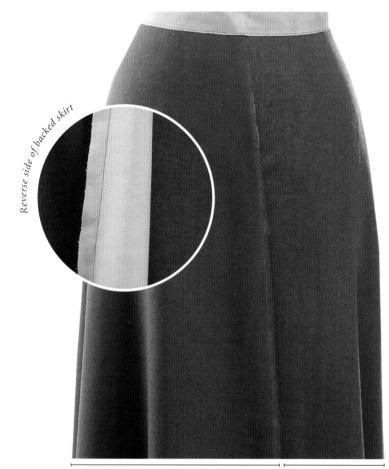

Reverse side of backed skirt

| Backed half of skirt | Unbacked half of skirt |

LIGHTWEIGHT WOOL BACKED WITH CHALLIS

The application of a rayon challis backing to the left-hand side of this lightweight wool skirt gives it greater depth, better drape and a wonderful hand. The skirt looks fuller and more relevant.

Reverse side of backed skirt

| Backed half of skirt | Unbacked half of |

LIGHTWEIGHT WOOL BACKED WITH VOILE

The left-hand side of this lightweight wool skirt is backed with voile. The voile helps to eliminate transparency and adds a slight perkiness to the overall appearance.

Silk Velvet

Silk velvet, an absolutely stunning fabric. Unbacked silk velvet has the most drape and movement; backing is not required for a full, fluid skirt. However, if you wanted to make a more fitted skirt or a matching jacket, backing fabrics would prove worthy assistants. In the examples below, the right-hand sides of the skirts are left unbacked for contrast.

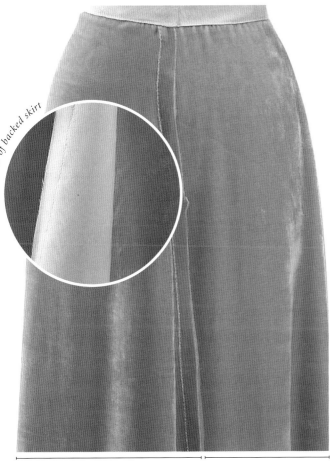

Reverse side of backed skirt

...ue of backed skirt

| *Backed half of skirt* | *Unbacked half of skirt* |
| *Backed half of skirt* | *Unbacked half of skirt* |

SILK VELVET BACKED WITH SILK ORGANZA

It is difficult to place pattern markings directly onto velvet, and a backing fabric provides the perfect vehicle for this process. Backing silk velvet with pre-washed silk organza (left-hand side) allows you to make all the necessary markings on the organza before backing the velvet; it also removes the 'crispness' of the silk velvet.

SILK VELVET BACKED WITH COTTON BATISTE

Backing silk velvet skirt with cotton batiste (left-hand side) offers a soft, stable layer between the body and the garment. This does not detract from the velvet's inherent drape but may provide a 'smoothing' layer over figure irregularities, perhaps in a pair of smart trousers, for example.

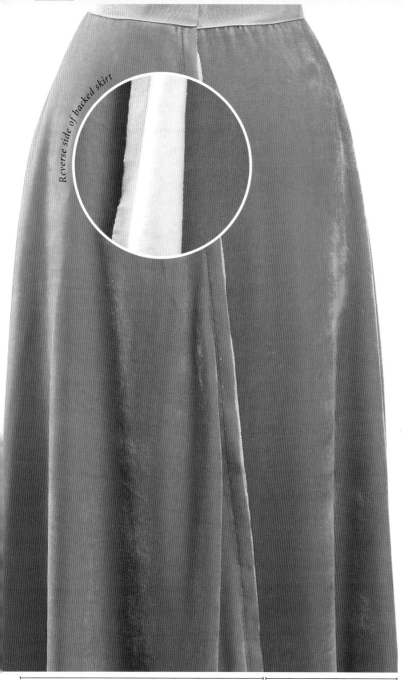

Reverse side of backed skirt

| Backed half of skirt | Unbacked half of skirt |

Silk Charmeuse

Silk charmeuse is a beautiful and luxurious fabric. It is incredibly versatile, and so are the companion fabric possibilities. The unadulterated version is perfect for lingerie, blouses, tank tops and flowing dresses. If you want to create a pair of trousers, an interlining would help the charmeuse to skim the figure gracefully, smoothing any irregularities. In the examples below, the right-hand sides of the skirts are left unbacked for contrast.

Reverse side of backed skirt

| Backed half of skirt | Unbacked half of skirt |

SILK VELVET BACKED WITH COTTON FLANNEL

In this example the silk velvet is interlined with cotton flannel (left-hand side), which adds weight and substance. Another assistance provided by the backing fabric is as a housing for tacked-down seam allowances. Velvet is difficult to press and you may choose to catch-stitch the seam allowances to an interlining (in a coat or jacket for example) to maintain a well-pressed, refined appearance.

SILK CHARMEUSE BACKED WITH COTTON BATISTE

The cotton batiste interlining on the left-hand side of this example lends some 'stand-out' power and a fuller appearance to the silk charmeuse, while maintaining drape.

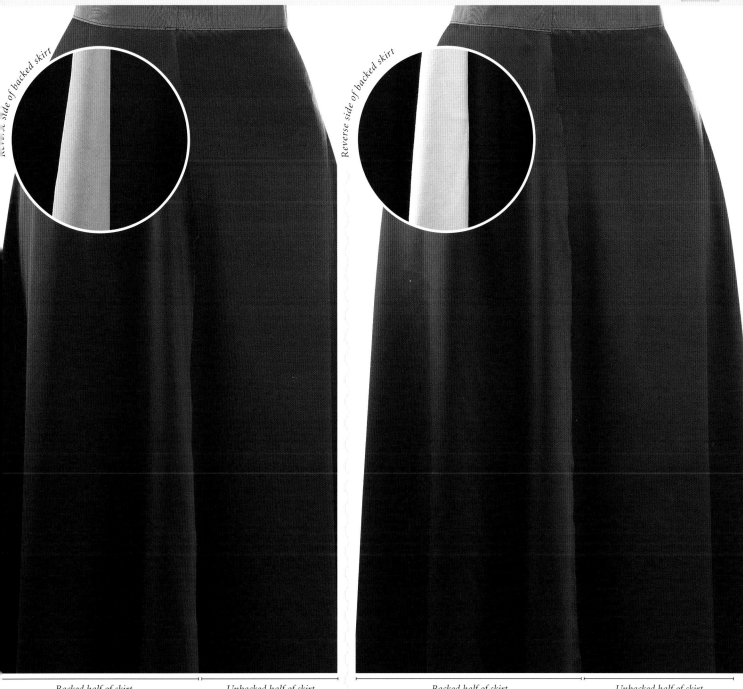

Reverse side of backed skirt

Reverse side of backed skirt

Backed half of skirt | Unbacked half of skirt

Backed half of skirt | Unbacked half of skirt

SILK CHARMEUSE BACKED WITH CRÊPE DE CHINE

The left-hand side of this silk charmeuse skirt is backed with
crêpe de chine, which maintains the same carefree drape as
the unbacked version, but with a more sumptuous hand and
a richer look.

SILK CHARMEUSE BACKED WITH RAYON CHALLIS

This sample skirt employs rayon challis as an interlining
on the left-hand side. The result is maximum drape
accompanied by loft and fluidity – over-the-top decadence.
Charmeuse is a fabric that presents a challenge when
marking design details. You must be careful with it; pins
may snag or otherwise mar the fabric.

CHAPTER FIVE

DIRECTORY OF LUXURY FABRICS

This helpful directory introduces the luxury fabrics and trims used in the techniques showcased in this book. The major players (face fabrics) and the minor players (support fabrics) all deserve honourable mention, along with a detailed description of their practical points and some handy tips. This general resource will enlighten the seamster as to various functions and applications.

Choosing fabrics

Fabrics make all the difference. Quality,
compatibility and hand are necessary
considerations of great design.
*Giorgio Armani, Spring/Summer 2007
Fashion Show, Haute Couture, Paris*

LININGS

The lining covers the inside of a garment, allowing it to slide on and off more easily and making it more comfortable to wear. It conceals the raw edges, facings and interlinings as well as extending the life of the garment and improving the finished effect. A lining is cut from the pattern pieces of the main garment and made up as an independent piece before being sewn into place. Generally it is sewn to completely cover the inside of a piece of clothing. Choose sumptuous fabrics to line a couture garment and give a luxury finish.

SILK CRÊPE DE CHINE

Description: Silk crêpe de chine is a soft, crêpe-textured fabric in a plain weave that is available in a range of weights, making it a versatile material. It is popular as a fabric – with its soft, lustrous quality – but is also useful as a lining and an interlining to add depth and body to other fabrics.

Applications: Silk crêpe de chine is ideal for making dresses, shirts, blouses, jackets and trousers when used as a fashion fabric. It makes a soft and comfortable lining while at the same time hiding the internal construction of a garment. It adds density

without structure when used as an interlining, allowing the main fabric to retain a 'soft' quality (if that property is required). Silk crêpe de chine works well as an interlining for a garment itself made from crêpe de chine, increasing the weight of a garment. Alternatively, use it to interline silk charmeuse (see page 114).

Practical points: Crêpe de chine can be difficult to cut as it tends to slide on a smooth cutting surface and shrink away from scissor blades. Reduce this effect by covering the tabletop with a cotton sheet and lay the crêpe de chine in a single layer on top. The short fibres in the cotton will help to hold the crêpe de chine in place. Use a fine size 9/70 standard or Microtex needle when sewing and choose French or flat fell seams to give a strong and neat finish.

Tips: Pre-launder the crêpe de chine interlining and the fashion fabric before sewing with them – they may have different rates of shrinkage and this may cause problems after construction of the garment.

ACETATE SATIN

Description: Acetate fibre is produced from wood pulp or cotton linters, chemically combined with acetic acid and extruded to form a fine filament. When spun into yarn and woven in a satin weave a fine, but weighty, fabric with a glossy surface is achieved. It drapes well, absorbs moisture and takes dyes easily, making it a useful material that was originally intended as a cheaper alternative to silk.

Applications: Acetate satin is used for blouses and dresses; its luxurious, shiny finish makes it especially suitable for eveningwear. It is ideal for lining garments because its absorbency makes it comfortable to wear next to the skin and the smooth satin weave allows it to slide on and off the body easily. Use it to line coats, jackets, skirts, trousers and dresses.

Practical points: Use sharp-bladed scissors when cutting acetate satin and cut in a single layer, because the smooth surfaces slide over one another when folded. Sew with a fine size 9/70 standard or Microtex

Linings and interlinings

Often the choice of the interlining will be
predetermined as a result of the fashion
fabric choice. This doesn't mean you should
be led entirely by the functionality of a fabric.
Always consider whether your lining will be
visible and choose a fabric that will either
pass unnoticed, keeping the focus on the
external design, or choose a fabric that will
bring a new design edge to a garment. If you
love brightly patterned linings but don't want
to ruin your design aesthetic, consider
keeping them for pocket linings and other
'secret' finishes known only to the wearer.

*Manish Arora, Autumn/Winter 2006, London
Fashion Week*

machine needle and choose a good-quality polyester thread to sew with. When machining, gently pull the fabric in front of and behind the needle. This, in conjunction with the polyester thread, will keep the seams from puckering. Iron with a press cloth on a well-padded surface to avoid ridges showing on the right side of the fabric parallel to seams and hems.

Tips: Acetate lining shows perspiration stains so it needs to be laundered frequently. Dry-clean, hand-wash or use a warm machine-wash (max. 40°C/104°F) and short spin to prevent permanent creasing.

SILK CRÊPE DE CHINE
See Linings, page 118.

SILK CHARMEUSE
See Luxury fabrics, page 125.

INTERLININGS

Interlining is an extra layer of fabric placed against the wrong side of a garment to add support or change the characteristics of the fashion fabric. Unlike interfacing, which adds support to small areas of a garment, interlining is mounted on the underside of the fabric across an entire area. The interlining is cut out exactly the same as each pattern piece and then hand-tacked to the wrong side of the dress fabric. These combined pieces are then treated as one when the garment is constructed. This process is different from lining and the finished interlined garment might well be lined, as well. Choose interlinings with the characteristics required to create a particular finish in a garment.

RAYON CHALLIS

Description: Rayon was created at the end of the 1900s from wood pulp as a cheaper alternative to silk. It is comfortable to wear and does not pill or build up static although it does fray easily. Rayon challis is a soft, light cloth, making it ideal as an interlining to add body and depth to a garment without creating excess bulk.

Applications: Use rayon as a fashion fabric for skirts, dresses and trousers – although it is best to avoid close-fitting styles. Use rayon challis as an interlining for garments where some support is required to maintain the shape and also to lengthen the garment's life. When used as an interlining, rayon challis can stabilize the outer fabric and make construction easier. Use it to back a lightweight wool skirt to add greater depth, give better drape and improve the handling qualities.

Practical points: Rayon challis is easy to handle, making cutting and sewing trouble-free. Cut out with sharp scissors and use fine pins within the seam allowance. Sew with a size 9/70 standard or Microtex machine needle with a stitch length of 2.5mm (10 stitches per inch). Use the challis as a 'skeleton' when hemming the garment, so that any hand stitches will be invisible from the right side of the finished item.

Tips: Pre-shrink the rayon challis and the outer fashion fabric before cutting out and hand-tacking the panels together.

BATISTE

Description: Batiste is a soft and sheer plain-woven fabric similar to lawn and organdy but slightly heavier. Named after the French weaver, Jean Batiste, this delicate fabric is associated with quality. It can be produced from cotton, cotton/polyester mix, linen, all synthetic fibres, wool and even silk. It is generally available in white, ivory and black and sometimes pastel shades, because it is a suitable weight for summer dress wear.

Applications: Use cotton batiste for heirloom sewing to decorate lingerie, nightwear and christening gowns. Cotton and linen batiste are suitable for summer dresses and tops. As an interlining, cotton batiste is ideal for backing other fabrics for garments since it is an appropriate weight and its natural fibre makes it 'breathable' and hence more comfortable to wear. It therefore supports the fashion cloth without adding density. It is also ideal for interlining quilts.

Practical points: When cutting out batiste use long, fine pins within the seam allowance and, if the fabric has been folded on the bolt, avoid using the fold as it may be permanently creased. Stay-stitch necklines and off-grain edges before sewing up, because the fabric may stretch and distort. Sew this fine fabric with a shorter stitch (2mm/12 stitches per inch) and use a size 9/70 standard or Microtex needle, although a size 11/80 needle may be better if it is used to interline a heavier cloth. If a straight stitch presser foot is available use it when straight-stitching batiste to prevent the soft and fine cloth from being pulled down into the

workings of the machine. Delicate French seams are a neat option.

Tips: Before working heirloom techniques on cotton batiste, use spray starch to stiffen the cloth and make handling easier. When machining, gently pull the fabric in front of and behind the presser foot to ease the fabric through and prevent wrinkling.

VOILE

Description: Voile is a sheer, transparent fabric constructed in a plain weave, which is both thin and light. It is similar to cotton lawn and batiste but the fibres are highly spun and this gives a crisper finish. It was traditionally made from cotton but synthetics are now frequently used for voile especially for home furnishing projects.

Applications: Synthetic voiles are popular as window dressings. Cotton and cotton-mix voiles are more often used for dressmaking projects such as blouses and dresses, although they do need to be lined. Voile is often printed to match a heavier weight of fabric and these are suitable for casual jackets and wraps worn with a matching print dress. Cotton voile can be used for antique or heirloom sewing and it makes a useful interlining material, adding stability and crispness to the outer fabric.

Practical points: Cut voile in a single layer and place it on a work surface covered with a cotton bedsheet to keep the voile from slipping and moving while cutting. Use weights or long, fine pins and cut with sharp shears for a clean edge. Sew with a fine size 9/70 standard or Microtex needle and short stitch length of 2mm (12 stitches per inch). Use French seams or hairline seams to join panels. When voile is used as an interlining, tack it to the wrong side of the fashion fabric with silk thread and treat the resulting pieces as the combined weight. This may mean using a larger needle and standard stitch length.

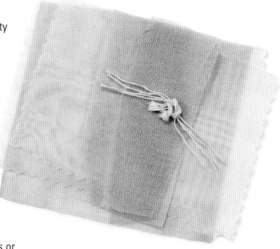

Tips: When interlining, hand-wash voile and the outer fashion fabric it is to be backed to, to pre-shrink them before constructing the garment.

SILK ORGANZA

Description: Silk organza is a fine and sheer woven fabric that is strong and fairly stiff to handle. The long silk fibres are tightly spun to give the threads their strength before they are woven together. The resulting organza is transparent and crisp, and springy.

Applications: Although suitable for eveningwear, in the context of couture, silk organza is more often used as an interlining. Its stiff finish makes it ideal for supporting weaker fabrics when placed against the wrong side of the cloth. Use it to interline a straight skirt to prevent seating, or in the knees of trousers to keep them from bagging. It can also be used in delicate silk sleeves to hold the shape, or as interlining in a full bridal skirt to reduce creasing.

Practical points: Cut organza with sharp scissors or use pinking shears to prevent fraying. Tack the organza to the underside of the outer fabric using short lengths of silk thread for hand stitching – this is easier to work with than synthetic thread because it does not tangle. It is important to contour the organza interlining when it is hand-tacked to the fabric so that it fits around the body within the outer shell without wrinkling. When machine-stitching organza on its own, choose a fine size 9/70 needle for best results. If sewing it when fixed to another layer as interlining, use a needle suitable for sewing the outer fabric.

Tips: Do not use a polyester organza for interlining because it does not have the same properties as 100 per cent silk organza. Another use of 100 per cent silk organza is as a press cloth. It will not burn under the heat of the iron and its transparent quality allows you to see the garment beneath.

COTTON FLANNEL

Description: Cotton flannel is a light- to medium-weight woven fabric with a brushed finish, on one or both sides, giving it a warm feel and creating a napped surface. It has all the qualities of cotton, including absorbency, with a soft, warm surface and added depth created by the raised surface.

Applications: Use cotton flannel for bedding, pyjamas and nightgowns in colder climates. Consider choosing it to interline garments like jackets and coats where depth and warmth are required. Use it to back a fine silk evening jacket to add body and weight to the style and make it warmer to wear. The tiny cotton fibres on the surface of the flannel will adhere to the slippery silk and the two layers will work well together when being handled and sewn.

Practical points: Cotton flannel is an undemanding fabric to work with, being of stable woven construction and easily controlled by finger pressing or with the heat of an iron. The brushed fibres on the surface create a nap, making it essential to cut all fabric pieces in the same direction. Use long, fine pins and sew with a standard size 11/80 sewing machine needle and cotton thread if possible. Join the flannel interlining to the outer fashion fabric with short lengths of silk thread sewn as a running stitch within the seam allowance. The silk is less likely to knot and is easier to sew with.

Tips: Try to match the colour of the flannel to the outer fabric when using it as an interlining, because the tiny fibres may brush off onto the fashion fabric. As always, pre-shrink both interlining and fashion fabric before starting to cut out and sew.

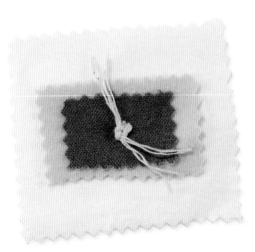

Unusual uses for lining fabrics

Lining fabrics such as silk organza need not be confined to the barely visible design solutions – use them anywhere you will get a 'flash' of lining fabric. You can also layer these lighter-weight fabrics on the exterior of a garment to create complex textures and ruffles without adding too much additional weight.

John Galliano for Christian Dior, Spring/ Summer 2009, Haute Couture, Paris Fashion Week

CALICO

Description: Calico is a stable, plain-woven cotton cloth. It is an inexpensive, practical cloth that does not have a particularly smooth finish. It is generally natural in colour, although it can be bleached. A range of weights and qualities is available.

Applications: Calico is used to make mock garments to test fit before making up the finished design. A test garment is often referred to as a 'toile', from a French word meaning 'linen cloth' ('muslin' is the term used in the United States). Calico is functional rather than decorative and is used for covering cushions and as an underlayer for soft furnishings such as chairs and sofas. It is useful for interlining clothing, adding depth, body and stability to a garment.

Practical points: Calico is a stable woven fabric ranging from light- to medium-weight, making it easy to handle and sew. No special cutting instructions are required as it has no nap or direction and cuts easily with sharp scissors. Use a size 11/80 standard needle to sew a 2.5mm (10 stitches per inch) stitch length and choose plain seams, pressed open, for a flat finish. When used with a fashion fabric as an interlining, treat and sew each panel as for the combined weight of fabrics.

Tip: Pre-shink calico before using, especially if it is going to be used as an interlining and the finished item will be laundered. Choose good quality calico, because cheaper lengths are 'sized' to add bulk and improve handling but this washes out when laundered.

HAIR CANVAS

Description: Hair canvas is a stiff, woven fabric traditionally made from wool, goat's hair and horse hair (sometimes blended with rayon, cotton or polyester). It is available in light, medium and heavy weights and is suitable for combining with various different fashion fabrics.

Applications: Hair canvas is commonly used in traditional tailoring to create moulded support and give shape to a garment. It is used in jacket construction to sculpt a good collar shape or to keep the chest/front shoulder area from collapsing under the weight of a shoulder bag or seatbelt. Slim-fitting winter woollen coats benefit from an interlining of hair canvas to support the shape and it also provides additional warmth. Even on a lighter-weight silk dupioni fabric, hair canvas is a useful backing, giving the necessary support to a 'stand out' design such as an A-line skirt.

Practical points: When using hair canvas as an interlining, cut off the hem allowance, lap the seams, and slash open and lap darts to reduce bulk. Cut hair canvas on the bias when using it to interface a collar and create a centre back seam, because this allows it to be sculpted into shape with the help of hand-sewn pad stitching. Lap the two collar pieces together or cut the centre back without a seam allowance and hand stitch to join, thus preventing the bulk of a traditional plain seam. Hand-sew hair canvas with a short, fine betweens needle and use silk thread to avoid knotting or tangling.

Tips: Use hair canvas in garments that require dry-cleaning.

LIGHTWEIGHT FUSIBLE INTERFACING FOR KNITS

Description: This light and sheer, knitted polyester fabric has a fusible film on one side. This allows it to be fixed to the wrong side of a knitted fashion fabric using the pressure, steam and heat of an iron. It is soft and light and adds body to the outer cloth without restricting its stretch.

Applications: Apply lightweight fusible interfacing to stretch-knit fabrics or to woven materials containing elastane. Once fused to the underside of the fashion cloth, the two layers will hold fast together and move as one. Use it to support small areas of a garment or to interline whole panels. It is useful when extra body and depth is required in the jacket of a suit while still matching the skirt or dress in terms of look. (In fact, the skirt or dress may need a different type of interlining to achieve the correct finish.)

Practical points: Cut the fusible interfacing 6mm (¼") smaller than each panel to keep it from sticking to the ironing board. Place the fashion fabric face down on the ironing board and cover with the fusible interfacing, with the 'glue' side facing down. Hold the iron above the fabric layers, applying steam without pressure over the entire area. This will cause shrinkage to occur and the interfacing will visibly bubble and move. Rearrange the interfacing over the fabric and now carefully press the weight of the iron over the two fabrics to fuse them together. Hold the iron in place for approximately 10 seconds to ensure the layers are fused. If creases appear, lift off while still warm and reapply.

Tips: Use a piece of silk organza as a press cloth when applying the fusible interfacing to protect the surface of the fabric. Store fusible interfacing on a roll to prevent it from creasing. It is not possible to iron it flat before use since the fusible film will melt and stick to the ironing board.

LUXURY FABRICS

Selecting elegant, luxurious fabrics for couture creations is essential. Couture sewing takes time and effort and is only worthwhile on the best-quality and richest materials. Never compromise on the fabric, because no amount of handling will make up for it. Treat it with respect, storing it carefully without creasing it; out of light and away from moisture.

SILK CHARMEUSE

Description: Silk charmeuse has a very soft feel with a shiny surface and a matte back. The satin weave construction means that long threads lie on the surface, giving the characteristic glossy finish. It drapes beautifully and catches the light, giving the impression of extravagance and luxury.

Sheer drape

Luxury couture fabrics can bring out the best in your garments, unlocking new design potential in tried and tested dress-pattern shapes. The classic empire-line dress shown here, uses fabric to bring the design to its zenith. Layered, floating fabrics are often balanced by a more structured element, such as the sequined bodice shown here – the toned-down colour palette completes the focus on the fabric. With layers of sheer fabric no lining is required – although you may prefer to add one to avoid static build-up. For single layers of sheer fabrics the lining fabric will be visible, opening up a host of design options for layering sheer and opaque colours.

Kevan Hall, Autumn/Winter 2005, Mercedes Benz Fashion Week, Los Angeles

Applications: Use silk charmeuse for special-occasion and eveningwear, where a soft drape and luxury sheen are required – for example in long, flowing dresses. Its soft feel makes it perfect for clothing worn next to the skin such as blouses, lingerie and also for linings. Use it to line jackets, skirts and dresses and to make bound edges on necklines and armholes.

Practical points: The soft and supple handle of silk charmeuse makes it difficult to cut out, because it slides away from the shears and inaccurate cutting can result. For best results place a length of cotton sheeting on the work surface and lay the charmeuse in a single layer on top to keep it from shifting, then cut through both layers. When cutting bias strips to make binding, use a rotary cutter with a ruler and a self-healing mat below to get straight edges. Pin only within the seam allowances as pin-holes may remain, and use a very fine size 9/70 machine needle (standard or Microtex). Sew with silk thread if possible and shorten the stitch length to 2mm (12 stitches per inch). French seams or plain seams (pressed open) are a good choice. Press with a dry iron to avoid water marks and use a press cloth to protect the surface of the fabric. The surface fibres of the satin weave are delicate and can be damaged or snagged, so keep silk charmeuse fabric for special garments rather than everyday wear.

Tips: Dry-clean garments that are made from, or lined with, silk charmeuse to prolong the life of the fabric.

HAMMERED SATIN

Description: Made from silk or synthetic fibres, hammered satin has a bumpy, textured finish similar in appearance to hammered metal. The sheen of the satin finish has more depth and volume as a result. This fabric has a lustrous appearance and a soft handle that drapes well due to the weight in the cloth.

Applications: Silk hammered satin is perfect for couture gowns. Use it for dresses, skirts and blouses. It looks sumptuous and drapes well, making it appropriate for special-occasion or eveningwear.

Practical points: Silk and rayon hammered satin both drape well and are relatively easy to sew, while the polyester variety is lighter in weight, more difficult to stitch and handles less easily. On a satin fabric the light catches the surface reflecting it in different ways depending on the direction of the grain. This makes it essential that all pattern pieces are cut in the same direction otherwise colour differences between panels will be evident. Cut with sharp scissors for a neat edge and hold in place with long, sharp pins. Sew with a new, fine size 9/70 standard or Microtex needle. The surface fibres of the satin are easily snagged by a dull needle and this will damage the appearance of the fabric. Shorten the stitch length to 2mm (12 stitches per inch) and gently support the fabric in front of and behind the needle when machining to keep the seams from puckering. Construct garments with French or plain seams and sew hems and facings in position, catching the stitches to the interlining (if there is one) for an invisible finish.

Tips: Use a press cloth and light pressure when ironing hammered silk to protect its surface.

SILK DUPIONI

Description: This crisp, woven fabric has an uneven surface created by slubs in the silk yarn. Both front and back look alike. It creases easily, but this can be reduced if you use a suitable interlining.

Applications: Choose silk dupioni for eveningwear and bridalwear. It is suitable for dresses, trousers, skirts, jackets and hats. The characteristics of silk dupioni can be altered depending on the interlining you use. A backing of cotton flannel will add depth and weight to a silk dupioni skirt, reducing its crispness, making it appear softer and improving its drape (see page 111).

Practical points: The colour of silk dupioni can vary depending on how the light hits it, so cut all pattern pieces in the same direction (as if for a nap). Use sharp shears and pin within the seam allowance. Silk dupioni is easy to handle and sew but it does tend to fray badly – trim seams with pinking shears to reduce fraying if the garment will be lined, or use a Hong Kong finish (see page 59). This fabric responds well to the heat of the iron, although a steam iron may cause watermarks. Use the iron as a sewing aid and to reduce the need to pin or tack hems and edges. Sew with a standard stitch length of 2.5mm (10 stitches per inch) and a fine size 9/70 machine needle. Choose fine cotton or silk thread and plain seams.

Tips: The front and back of the fabric look alike, so mark the wrong side with tailor's chalk before making up a garment.

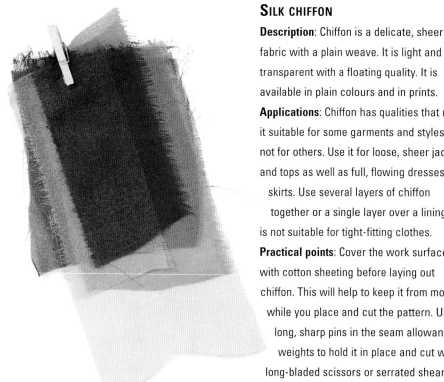

SILK CHIFFON

Description: Chiffon is a delicate, sheer fabric with a plain weave. It is light and transparent with a floating quality. It is available in plain colours and in prints.

Applications: Chiffon has qualities that make it suitable for some garments and styles but not for others. Use it for loose, sheer jackets and tops as well as full, flowing dresses and skirts. Use several layers of chiffon together or a single layer over a lining. It is not suitable for tight-fitting clothes.

Practical points: Cover the work surface with cotton sheeting before laying out chiffon. This will help to keep it from moving while you place and cut the pattern. Use long, sharp pins in the seam allowance or weights to hold it in place and cut with long-bladed scissors or serrated shears. Sew with a fine sharp needle (size 9/70) and shorten the stitch length to 1.5–2mm (13–15 stitches per inch). Sew chiffon with silk thread. Use narrow French or hairline seams for a delicate join. If a straight stitch foot and plate are available, use them for sewing to prevent the fine fabric from being pulled down below the stitch plate into the mechanism. Finish hems with a delicate rolled hem sewn by hand, or overlock a picot edge. Interline or interface chiffon with chiffon to add body without detracting from its sheer, transparent quality. Alternatively, interline with a natural-coloured organza for greater stiffness. Buttonholes can be stabilized with a small piece of silk organza, then trimmed to a minimum when sewn.

Tip: If a roll of medical examination paper is available, use this as a base when cutting out chiffon, and cut through both layers.

HANDKERCHIEF LINEN

Description: Handkerchief linen is linen of the very lightest quality. It is a fine, lightweight fabric woven in a plain weave

from the longest linen fibres. It is almost translucent, soft to the touch and has a smooth surface finish.

Applications: Apart from its traditional use for handkerchiefs, this lightweight linen is ideal for children's clothing, ladies' blouses and men's shirts. It is perfect for summer wear and lingerie items as it is so soft, light and absorbent. Choose handkerchief linen for heirloom sewing projects.

Practical points: Cut with long-bladed shears and, if the fabric length has been folded, avoid this crease because it may be

permanent. Use long pins and sew with a fine, standard needle size 9/70. Reduce the machine stitch length to 2mm (12 stitches per inch) and choose narrow French seams for a delicate finish. Fit a straight stitch foot and plate to the sewing machine when straight stitching. Interface and interline with a second layer of handkerchief linen for more support if necessary.

Tips: Hand-wash handkerchief linen and do not over-spin. Iron while it is still damp for a smooth finish.

LIGHTWEIGHT KNITS

Description: Lightweight knitted fabric varies depending on the fibre it is made from, but all types will have a degree of stretch because of the loop construction of the yarns. Some slinky knits have a lustre and lend themselves to elegantly draped designs. Others, made from cotton fibres, have a little more stability though the cut edges will still tend to curl.

Applications: Use lightweight knits for tops, cardigans and delicate unstructured jackets, skirts, dresses and trousers. The stretch of a lightweight knit may do away with the need for other closures and fastenings. Some lightweight knits may need the stability of an interlining to give more structure to a garment.

Practical points: When cutting out, consider the direction of stretch since there is no grain. Join seams on a lightweight knit with an overlocker, because this copes well with the stretch in the cloth. If using a sewing

machine, select a pre-programmed stretch stitch or a narrow zigzag and fit a walking foot for best results. The walking foot prevents the rippling that sometimes occurs when stitching a stretch fabric. Sew seams with a stretch or ballpoint needle and sew a topstitched hem with a 4mm twin (or double) needle. The parallel rows of stitching on the surface are linked with one thread below from the bobbin and this gives a degree of stretch so the thread in the seams will not break when pulled. Stabilize buttonholes with a square of silk organza between the fabric and facing to add support. Use lightweight fusible interfacing designed for knits if necessary.

Tip: A lightweight knit will curl at the edges, iron with spray starch to reduce this tendency (try this on a scrap of fabric first to check that the fabric will not be adversely affected by the starch).

Velvet

An intensely luxurious fabric with timeless appeal, velvet is available in numerous colours and weights. It suits simple pattern shapes, and constructions with few seams that allow the fabric to be shown to its greatest effect. If velvet is allowed to drape around the body you will get contrasting areas of deep colour versus shimmering sheen as the fabric's pile shifts in the light. *Bottega Veneta, Autumn/Winter 2009, Milan Fashion Week*

SILK VELVET

Description: Velvet is a woven fabric with a dense cut pile on its surface, making it a thick cloth. The fibres that create the deep pile catch the light in different ways depending on how the panels are cut. A rich colour is produced when the pile faces upwards but a lighter sheen is reflected when the pile is brushed downwards. The latter wears better as the pile fibres are smoothed flat rather than being squashed and damaged.

Applications: Silk velvet makes beautiful, sumptuous clothing with a rich, luxury appeal. Use it for jackets, evening bodices, dresses and trousers. With appropriate interlining silk velvet can be used for many different purposes. It can be given more structure with a stiff silk organza interlining or the soft drape retained, but supported, with a softer cotton lawn.

Practical points: Lay pattern pieces all in the same direction to avoid shading differences. Cut with the pile downwards for good wear or upwards for a richer colour. Use long, sharp pins placed within the seam allowance. Sew with a standard size 11/90 needle and lengthen the stitch to 3mm (8 stitches per inch). Fit a walking foot to the sewing machine and sew in the direction of the pile. When attaching lining, sew with the lining on top and the velvet below to avoid 'creeping'. Iron velvet lightly, with the right side down on a velvet board or a separate piece of velvet to keep the pile from being crushed. Do not topstitch silk velvet; choose concealed zips sewn into the seam, and loops rather than buttonholes. To finish, put the completed garment onto a tailor's form and steam with a tank iron without allowing the sole plate to touch the fabric surface. The tank iron produces strong bursts of steam that will help to remove any wrinkles.

Tips: Do not fold velvet during construction. Keep the fabric pieces flat. When cutting out, keep the vacuum cleaner handy to control the loose pile fibres.

LIGHTWEIGHT WOOL

Description: Lightweight wool includes fabrics like wool crepe, worsted wool and wool gauze or voile. They are finer and smoother in weight than other wools, which are recognized as being fluffier and more bulky. They have their individual characteristics but generally, as lightweight wool is less thick, it is comfortable to wear and easier to work with.

Applications: Wool gauze is a fine sheer cloth and good for blouses and dresses while worsted wool is more stable and suitable for jackets, trousers and skirts. The interesting texture and structure of wool crêpe makes it

appropriate for bias-cut designs as well as trousers, skirts and jackets.

Practical points: Sew lightweight wool with a standard-sized needle and use silk or polyester thread to sew it with because these have a slight 'give', which allows the stitches to move with the natural wool fabric. A standard stitch length of 2.5mm (10 stitches per inch) is most suitable.

Tips: For a luxury finish on a lightweight wool garment, finish the raw edges of the seam and hem with Hong Kong binding in a fine habotai silk.

COTTON BATISTE

See Batiste, page 121.

VOILE

See Interlining, page 121.

ORGANDY

Description: Organdy is a plain-woven fabric made from very fine, combed cotton threads. It is a very sheer, crisp cloth that creases easily, but modern finishes have been developed to reduce this problem. This

cotton fabric is similar in appearance and handle to silk organza.

Applications: Commonly used for blouses and shirts, but the crispness of the cloth determines the styles it is suited to. Use organdy for heirloom stitched projects or embellish it with sequins and embroidery. Organdy is perfect for summerwear because of its cotton fibre content and light weight.

Practical points: As there is no obvious right and wrong side to the fabric it is important to be consistent when cutting out and to mark the wrong side of each piece with tailor's chalk. The crispness of the fabric makes cutting fairly straightforward, but do use sharp shears and secure it with long, sharp pins placed within the seam allowance (to avoid visible holes). Stitch with a fine, standard needle (size 9/70) and reduce the stitch length to

2mm (12 stitches per inch). Use a straight stitch foot and plate and machine with fine cotton thread. For hand sewing choose silk thread. Interline organdy with more organdy to provide additional support without altering the sheer quality of the cloth. Construct garments with narrow French seams or hairline seams to give a delicate finish. Alternatively, use an overlocker set to a rolled hemstitch to join pieces of organdy. This gives a very fine seam with a subtle finish that is suitable for some parts of a garment although it does not have a great deal of strength.

Tips: If bias strips are required, cut organdy with a rotary cutter on a self-healing mat and use a patchworker's ruler for perfectly straight lines.

SILK GAZAR

Description: Silk gazar is similar to organza but is a slightly heavier weight with a stiffer feel due to an added 'size'. The fabric does not drape and this limits its potential for some styles. It is constructed in a plain weave with four-ply silk threads. It has a crisp texture and has been popular with designers since the 1960s.

Applications: Choose silk gazar for crisp blouses and shirts, dresses, skirts and loose coats. Use it for bridal gowns with full skirt designs.

Practical points: Cut out with long-bladed scissors and pin paper pattern pieces in place with long pins in the seam allowance.

Reduce the stitch length to 2mm (12 stitches per inch) and fit a fine or Microtex needle (size 9/70) for best results. Sew with silk or cotton machine thread and hand-sew with short lengths of silk to reduce knotting. Fit a straight stitch foot and plate to the machine and start sewing 3mm (⅛") in from the edge to prevent the fabric from being pulled down into the mechanism. Choose narrow French or hairline seams for a delicate finish. Use a press cloth to protect the surface of the cloth.

Tip: Pre-shrink silk gazar with steam from the iron and dry clean

when the garment is completed. Washing out the 'size' will reduce the stiffness of the cloth.

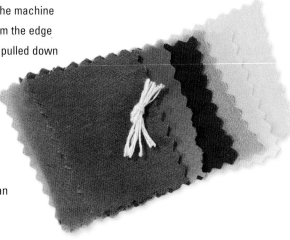

Sheers and sequins

Structured, sheer fabrics such as organdy or
silk gazar combine the delicate appeal of a
sheer fabric such as chiffon, but add their
own unique design possibilities with clean
lines and crisp edges. For a truly show-
stopping finish, consider embellishing your
garments with hand-stitched sequins or
beads. The safest place to start is with a type
of bead or sequin that perfectly matches the
colour of your fabric to avoid a garish finish.
Sequins can be built-up or 'massed' in a
particular area of a garment (such as the
collar and shoulders), gradually becoming
more spaced out down the garment to give
an overall effect that avoids hundreds of
hours of hand stitching.

*Valentino, Autumn/Winter 2009, Haute
Couture, Paris Fashion Week*

LINEN

Description: Linen is an ancient textile made from the stems of the flax plant, which are processed to release the fibres. These fibres are spun, then woven into a strong, crisp fabric. Handkerchief linen (see page 129) is a plain-woven lightweight fabric, while standard linen is medium to heavier weight and woven in plain, twill or damask weaves. All linen wrinkles and creases badly but it can be treated to reduce this problem.

Applications: Linen is suitable for blouses, shirts, jackets, coats and trousers depending on its weight. It is ideal for heirloom sewing because the woven threads respond well to drawn-thread work produced by hand or on a sewing machine. Although linen wrinkles badly, this is one of its recognizable characteristics and gives it its charm.

The natural absorbency of the linen fibres makes this a comfortable fabric to wear.

Practical points: Cut linen with shears and mark the wrong side of the cloth with tailor's chalk. Sew with good quality cotton thread and use a standard 2.5mm (10 stitches per inch) stitch length. For topstitching, use topstitching embroidery thread, which is thicker and looks pleasingly prominent on the surface of the finished garment. Choose a standard needle in a size appropriate for the weight of the linen (9/70 for handkerchief linen, 11/80 for medium-weight and 14/90 for heavier linen). Join linen with plain, flat fell or topstitched seams and hem with a twice-folded and topstitched hem. A twin needle, or a wing needle sewn with a blanket-style machine stitch, gives an attractive finish.

Tip: Pre-wash and iron or just press the entire length of cloth before cutting out. This will reduce the amount of wrinkling. While working with linen, use the iron as a tool to help fold the fabric into the correct position for stitching.

TRIMS

Ribbons, tapes and cords are used in couture sewing for functional reasons to support and protect areas within a garment or as laces/ties for closures. They can also be added as a decorative trim or finish to the surface. Cords may be sewn beneath the surface of a fabric to add a textured finish, or to the right side as embellishment along with ribbons and braids. As with all couture work, choose good quality trims to match the luxury fabrics.

RAYON RIBBON

Description: Rayon ribbon is a durable ribbon with a soft texture. Less shiny but softer and more pliable than satin ribbon it is comfortable when in contact with the skin.

Applications: Use rayon ribbon as a trim on the hem of a skirt or dress or to embellish sleeves, cuffs and collars. For more practical purposes, use it as a closure in the form of ties or to finish raw edges and zips on the inside of garments. It can also be used for hanging loops to hold a garment on a hanger.

Practical points: Sew rayon ribbon with a fine and sharp standard or Microtex needle (size 9/70). Choose a good colour-matched thread to sew with.

Tips: Cut the loose ends of rayon ribbon diagonally to prevent fraying and consider the laundering properties of the ribbon and fabric before combining them.

MOUSETAIL

Description: Mousetail is the same as rattail (see page 139), but is slightly narrower.

Applications: Use as rattail.

Practical points: Sew as rattail.

Tips: Use mousetail or rattail cord for turning through bias strips to make cord. The satin surface of the cord allows the bias strip to slide over it and turn through more easily.

STRING

Description: String, from any hardware shop, can be a useful product when sewing. It is thin and flexible, made from a variety of fibres and available in different thicknesses.

Applications: Use string in place of cord for piping or to turn lengths of rouleaux (narrow bias tubes) when making tiny straps or ties.

Practical points: Choose a soft string which will be pliable and easy to manipulate. Use an appropriate width for the task required.

Tips: Knot the end of the string in the bundle to prevent fraying. Pre-launder to shrink the string if using it in a washable item.

PETERSHAM

Description: Petersham ribbon is a stiff, closely woven tape with a pronounced edge. It comes in a variety of widths from 12mm (½") to 10cm (4") and may be straight or curved.

Applications: Petersham is often used to support the band of a waist in a skirt or a dress. It should fit the waist snugly and allow the garment to be anchored by it. A curved Petersham allows a waistband to tilt towards the upper body, giving a better fit. Petersham also provides a pretty detail when inserted into a flat fell seam with its edge peeking out of the finished, top-stitched seam (see page 56).

Practical points: The density of the weave makes Petersham difficult to pin, so strong, sharp pins are essential. When sewing Petersham in place it is easier to control if placed on the surface of the fabric rather than having the fabric on top. Sew with a standard size 11/80 needle and a stitch length of 2.5mm (10 stitches per inch). Edge-stitch both sides of the tape to hold it in place. Fold the ends of the Petersham under, and stitch down to finish the ends; add hooks and eyes for closures if you are using it as a waist stay.

Tips: Sew Petersham to the base of the crown on the inside of a hat to help keep its shape.

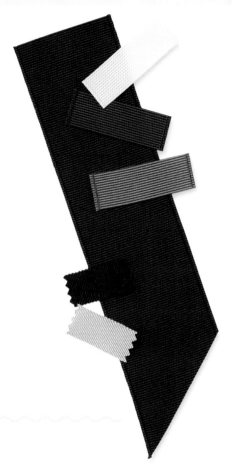

YARN

Description: There are many attractive, decorative yarns available for knitting and crochet that can also be used as trims for garments. These may be textured, bouclé, metallic or variegated and can be used either individually or mixed together. Plainer yarns have more functional uses, as cords when channel stitching (see page 52) or as soft piping cords.

Applications: Decorative yarns can be couched (sewn in place with additional threads) to fabric on collars, cuffs and hems. Braid can be created by sewing these fancy yarns onto a grosgrain ribbon then stitching the ribbon in place on a garment.

Practical points: Couch the yarns in place by hand or with a zigzag stitch wide enough to catch the yarns and hold them in place to the backing fabric. A braiding or cording foot will make this process easier. Choose a standard needle in an appropriate size to suit the fabric and a carefully colour-matched thread. Alternatively, use an invisible nylon thread, or even a metallic thread to give a sparkling effect. In the case of the latter, select a metallic needle to keep the thread from shredding.

Tips: Dry-clean the finished garment to prolong the life and texture of the fancy yarns. Pre-wash other yarns to shrink them before sewing with them.

Trimming and embellishing

Decorative trims and embellishments, such
as braids, ribbons and embroidery – with
or without beads and sequins – may be
added to a garment as one of the final
stages, but some details are added before
garment pieces are joined and lined to
conceal the stitching. In either case, the final
trimming must always be considered from the
outset. You can combine pieces of ribbon and
braid with strings of beads to create your
own custom trims to match a particular
fabric, or you may find it easier to start with
a trim and then choose a fabric which either
matches, or contrasts, perfectly.
Anna Sui, Spring/Summer 2005, Olympus
Fashion Week, New York

SATIN RIBBON

Description: Satin has a beautiful sheen due to its weave, in which the warp threads lie across the surface and reflect the light. Satin ribbon is available in a great variety of widths up to 7cm (3") and is primarily for decorative use. The main drawback of satin ribbon is that the surface threads are easily pulled and damaged. Grosgrain ribbon is more durable and is sometimes used as an alternative.

Applications: Use ribbon to decorate the inside of a collar band (see page 70), as a trim on the hem of a short sleeve, or sew several parallel rows of it above the hem of a skirt for added detail. On the inside of garments, satin ribbon is used to finish the edges of zip tape, as hanger loops on a skirt or as lingerie guards to control bra straps on the inside shoulder of a sleeveless dress.

Practical points: Sew satin ribbon with a fine and sharp standard or Microtex needle (size 9/70). A larger, or dulled, needle will pull the satin threads and mar the surface. Choose a carefully colour-matched thread and edge-stitch the ribbon into position.

Tips: Choose satin ribbon with the same fibre content as the garment it is to be sewn onto; choose silk satin ribbon rather than polyester to use on a silk garment.

GROSGRAIN RIBBON

Description: Grosgrain is a stiff, ribbed ribbon traditionally made from silk (although today it is more commonly made from rayon). It is available in various widths and has a characteristic vertical rib, which gives it rigidity. It is available in widths from 6mm (¼") to 38mm (1½"), making it suitable for a variety of uses.

Applications: Use grosgrain ribbon as a waist stay inside a dress to anchor the waist, or use it as a belt backing to add stiffness to a dress fabric or trim. For a simple waist finish, lap grosgrain over the raw edge of a skirt and edge-stitch in place. Fold the ribbon to the wrong side, then edge-stitch again to hold it down. Alternatively, use it as a decorative trim in place of satin ribbon – it wears better and is considered less flashy. Use it on the inside of the cuffs of trousers to protect the edge from wear.

Practical points: Stitch grosgrain ribbon close to the edges to hold it flat and in place. Sew with good-quality and colour-matched thread. Use a standard size 11/80 needle and a stitch length of 2.5mm (10 stitches per inch).

Tip: Pre-shrink grosgrain ribbon before sewing it into a garment.

RATTAIL

Description: Rattail is a tubular cord with a smooth, satin finish. It is available in many colours.

Applications: Use rattail to create a channel-stitching detail on a garment (see page 52) or couch coloured rattail in place with invisible threads for a decorative embellishment.

Practical points: When channel stitching use a twin needle to straddle the cord and a pintuck foot to keep the cords parallel. Use a standard stitch length of 2.5mm (10 stitches per inch) and good quality thread to match the colour of the fabric or cord.

Tip: When sewing with a twin needle leave the second thread out of the final guide just above the needle. This helps to keep the threads from knotting and tangling.

DECORATIVE TRIM

Description: Decorative trims include rickrack braid, piping cords with a flange, textured braids, and roses and bows that can be sewn onto garments as embellishments.

Applications: Use decorative trims to adorn garments whether they are tailored, outerwear items, or lingerie.

Practical points: Choose hand sewing, using a short, fine needle and silk thread to secure decorative trims or, if using a sewing machine, select an appropriate foot attachment. A zip foot will allow you to make stitches on the edge of a trim with the bulk or texture in the centre. Choose good quality thread in a colour close to that of the ribbon, or use invisible nylon thread.

Tip: Select trims to suit the fabric they are to be sewn onto, matching the fibre content, and opt for dry-cleaning rather than washing to prolong their life.

DECORATIVE RIBBON

Description: There is a huge range of decorative ribbons available for sewing. Plaid, moiré, striped, metallic, chiffon, velvet and novelty ribbons provide plenty of choice for embellishment of clothes.

Applications: Use decorative ribbons on the edges of collars or to trim cuffs or pockets. They may be used on a plain and simple design to create something more special.

Practical points: Sew decorative ribbons in place with a sewing machine using a straight stitch along each edge, or hand-sew in place with tiny catch stitches. Use a new and fine machine needle (9/70), considering the nature of the ribbon being sewn; a metallic needle may be necessary for some types. For hand-stitching choose a short, fine needle and silk thread.

Tips: When positioning ribbon before sewing, use very sharp pins and place them on the edges where the stitches will be made to avoid damaging the body of the ribbon.

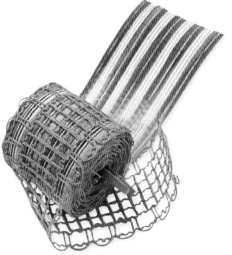

ESSENTIAL COUTURE TECHNIQUES

This guide to the essential couture techniques will take you through some of the more basic but nonetheless crucial know-how for the couture sewer. Techniques include the French seam, spaced tucks, interlining, buttons and buttonholes and useful refinements such as strengthening jacket cuffs stylishly with grosgrain ribbon.

Luxurious details

It is said that true luxury is like having
the mink on the inside of the garment. It's
these details that delight the wearer of
couture garments.

*Armani Prive Spring/Summer 2009, Paris
Haute Couture Fashion Week*

FRENCH SEAM

A French seam encloses the raw edges making additional finishing unnecessary. It looks flat like a plain seam from the front, but appears like a tuck on the reverse.

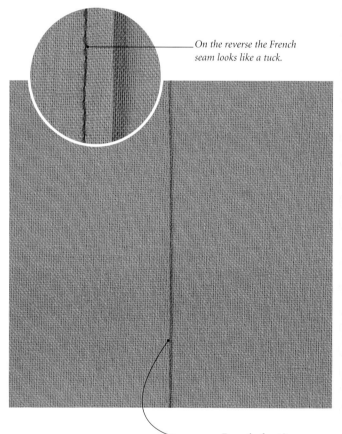

On the reverse the French seam looks like a tuck.

From the front it looks like a plain seam.

- Basic sewing supplies

1. Place the wrong sides of the fabric together, with the edges matching. Sew with a straight stitch 6mm (¼") from the edge.

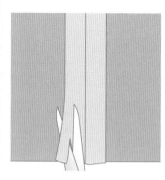

2. Press the seam open and trim the raw edges to approximately half.

3. Fold the seam the opposite way, so that the right sides are now together and the seam is pressed out to the edge.

4. Complete the seam with a final row of stitching 6mm (¼") from the edge. This will enclose all the raw edges.

Couture secrets

Adjust stitch length to suit the fabric: use a slightly longer stitch for thicker fabric and a slightly shorter one for finer material.

Use a French seam only for straight seams; it is too bulky for curves.

Make a mock French seam by sewing with the right sides together, then tuck the raw edges inwards and edge-stitch the seam allowances together.

Spaced Tucks

Spaced tucks are folds of cloth sewn at regular intervals to add texture and interest to a garment. Sew them in groups and down the full length of the tuck, or leave them free at one end. Use vertically on a bodice or yoke, or horizontally around the bottom of a skirt.

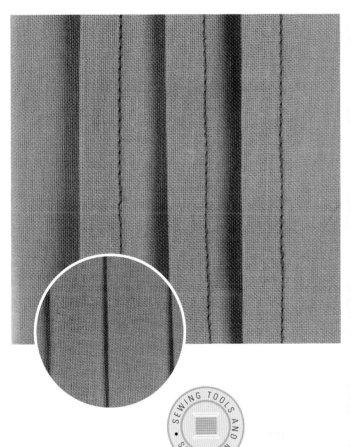

1. Mark the position and size of the tucks onto the fabric's surface.

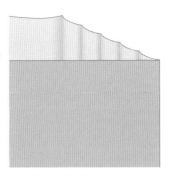

2. Fold the fabric along the lines with wrong sides together, and press with an iron.

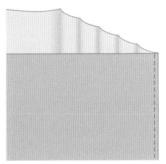

3. With a straight stitch, sew parallel to each of the folded edges to form the tucks.

4. When all the tucks have been completed, press them all in the same direction.

SEWING TOOLS AND MATERIALS

- Top-stitch foot
- Press cloth

HAND-FINISHED ZIP

A hand-finished zip is usually used in couture sewing. This method first applies the zip by machine for strength, but then finishes it with hand-stitching to make it special.

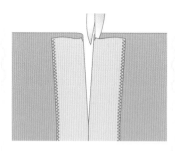

1. Make a plain seam where the zip is to be placed leaving the zip length unstitched. Finish the thread ends securely and press open. Mark the seam lines on the top edge with tiny snips.

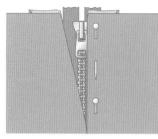

2. Place the zip face up on a work surface and position the open part of the seam allowance over it. Pin the right folded edge.

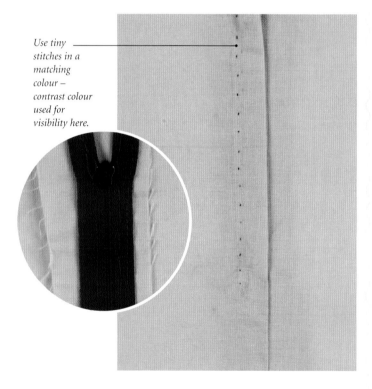

Use tiny stitches in a matching colour – contrast colour used for visibility here.

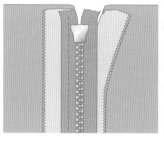

3. Flip over and re-pin the zip tape to the seam allowance only. Sew a line of straight stitching approximately 6mm (¼") from the teeth.

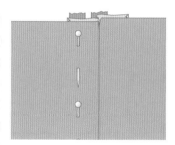

4. Turn to the right side and place the left folded edge over the teeth so that the seam line snips meet up. Pin the left edge.

SEWING TOOLS AND MATERIALS

- Zip
- Zip foot
- Silk thread

Couture secrets

Use silk thread for prick-stitching since it is less likely to tangle.

Cut short lengths of thread for hand-stitching to reduce knotting/tangling.

Closely made prick-stitches will be more noticeable.

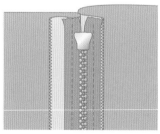

5. Flip over and re-pin the zip tape to the seam allowance only. Sew together using a line of straight machine stitches.

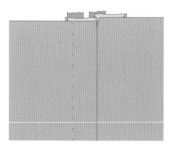

6. Turn to the right side again and pin through all layers on the left edge. Take tiny stitches from the bottom of the zip to the top keeping the stitches regular, but well spaced.

Adding a facing

To finish the top edge with a facing:

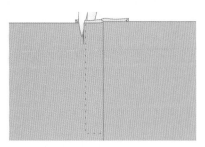

a) Snip the depth of the seam allowance at the seam line on the left edge;

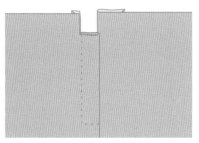

b) Fold this in and slip-stitch to close;

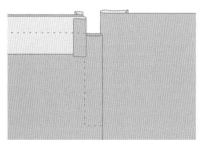

c) Attach the facing up to this point leaving space for the zip tab at the top edge.

INTERLINING

Interlining is applied directly to the underside of each fashion fabric piece before the garment is constructed.

- Interlining fabric
- Silk thread

1. Cut out each pattern piece in the chosen fabric as well as in a suitable interlining material such as habotai silk, silk organza or cotton lawn.

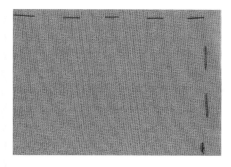

2. Pair up the pieces of interlining and chosen fabric with the wrong sides together. Pin around the outer edges.

3. With the chosen fabric uppermost, hand-tack this and the interlining together in the seam allowance. Note the edges will not match – the interlining is likely to appear larger than the upper fabric.

4. When sewn together, complete the garment as normal. The garment may still need to be lined in addition to this interlining.

HANGING LOOPS

These brilliantly designed hanging loops allow a skirt to be hung securely, but are cleverly hidden when worn (unlike traditional hanging loops which can sometimes be seen).

SEWING TOOLS AND MATERIALS

- Rotary cutter and mat
- Rouleau turner (loop turner)

1. Cut a bias length of lining fabric approximately 40cm (16") long and 2.5cm (1") wide.

2. Fold the strip in half and sew approximately 6mm (¼") from the fold. Turn through with a rouleau turner and cut the length in two.

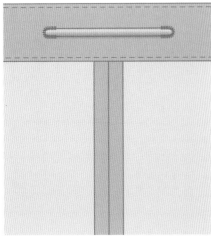

3. Tuck the ends inside and centre each length of rouleau over the side seams. Hand-sew each end securely in place.

4. Use the loops to hang the skirt, but notice how they disappear when the skirt fits around the body with no danger of them slipping out.

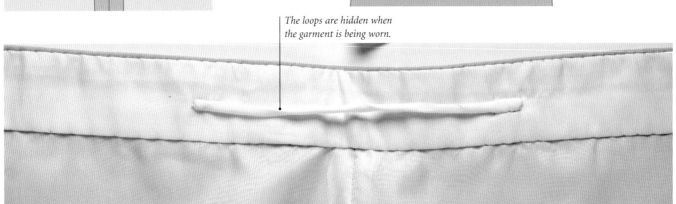

The loops are hidden when the garment is being worn.

ADDING GROSGRAIN RIBBON

Adding grosgrain ribbon or a tape on the inside lower edge of a cuff will protect the fabric from wear and tear.

The ribbon will protect the cuff from wear and tear.

1. Construct the cuff. Press the folds of the cuff into the hem to act as marker lines, then unfold the lower legs.

2. Place the tape on the inside of the cuff on the right side, just above the hem level. Pin, tack, then edge-stitch the tape in place.

3. The tape should be in the correct position to protect the inner cuff from wear from shoes.

SEWING TOOLS AND MATERIALS

- 15cm (6") ruler or measuring gauge
- 1.5cm (⅝") wide grosgrain ribbon or polyester tape

Sewing tip
Use this technique on all trousers – not just those finished with a cuff.

PIPED CUFF

Piping the edges of a cuff adds an attractive design detail and defines the outline. Use a fine piping cord, covered with the same fabric, or choose a contrasting colour.

- Piping cord
- Piping foot or adjustable zip foot

PREPARATION

Cut out the cuffs, facings and interfacings and fuse the interfacing to the wrong side of the cuffs.

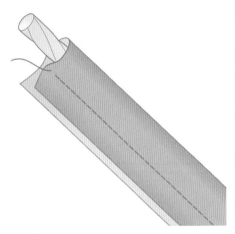

1. Cut a bias strip approximately 3cm (1¼") wide to cover the piping cord. Wrap the bias strip around the cord, and sew with a long straight stitch. The foot will allow the stitches to lie close to the cord.

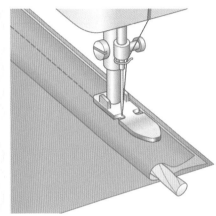

2. Place the wrapped cord to the edges of the cuff with all raw edges matching. Snip into the bias at the corners to allow it to lie smoothly. Pin, and tack if necessary, and then stitch in place.

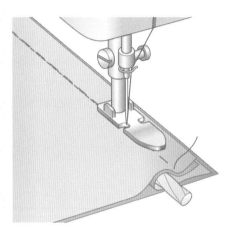

3. Apply the facing to the cuff and tack all layers together. Stitch from the cuff side to ensure that stitches are very close to the cord. Trim and layer the seam allowances and turn through.

Notes
- On fine fabrics, interline the bias strip with a layer of cotton lawn, also cut on the bias. This prevents any ridges in the cord from showing through.

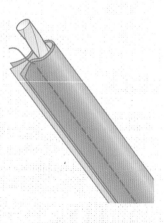

SHOESTRING STRAPS

Also known as spaghetti straps, these very fine straps are made by turning through a narrow strip of fabric and are often used in summer clothing and eveningwear.

SEWING TOOLS AND MATERIALS

- Rouleau turner (loop turner)

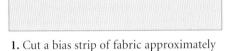

1. Cut a bias strip of fabric approximately 2.5cm (1") wide.

2. Fold this in half lengthways with the right sides together.

3. Shorten the stitch length and sew 6mm (¼") or less from the fold. Repeat with a second row of stitches to add strength. Do not trim the seam allowances.

4. Feed the rouleau turner into the strap and catch the opposite end. Pull through.

ALTERNATIVE

Make covered cord by wrapping a bias strip of fabric around a long length of cord (twice the length of the fabric strip). Using a zip foot, sew close to the cord and then through the cord at the end of the strip. Trim the seam allowances to a minimum and pull the fabric over the opposite half of the cord. Snip off the excess cord.

Sewing tip

Choose a satin fabric for shoestring straps since the smooth surface allows it to slide through and be turned more easily.

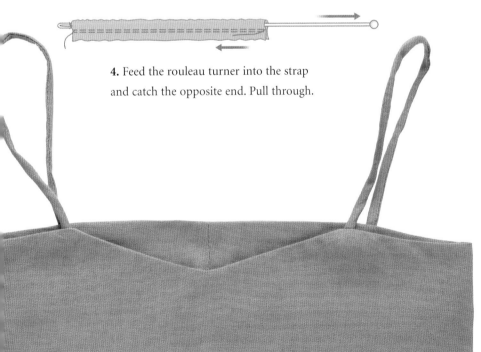

BUTTONS

Buttons generally come in three types: two-hole, four-hole and shank. When sewing on a button with holes, make a thread shank (see below) to accommodate the buttonhole's depth. Use strong thread and attach buttons to a double thickness of fabric. In the case of large buttons, sew a small plain one behind the larger one on the wrong side of the fabric to anchor it.

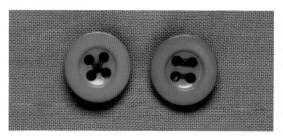

Buttons with holes.

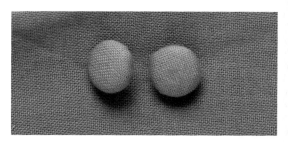

Covered shank buttons.

- Silk thread
- Buttonhole twist or strong thread

BUTTON WITH HOLES

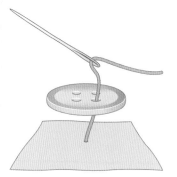

1. Secure the thread end in the fabric and take the needle up through one hole.

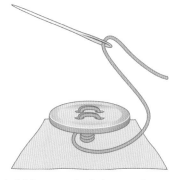

3. Make several stitches, as above, and bring the needle out between the button and fabric. Wind it around the loose central threads a few times to create a shank.

2. Take the needle back down through another hole and into the fabric leaving the thread loose, that is, keeping the button and fabric apart. Use a matchstick as a spacer if necessary.

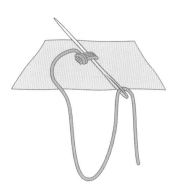

4. Take the needle through to the wrong side and loop through the threads to tie them together. Secure the thread end.

BUTTON WITH A SHANK

Sew as above, but take the needle directly through the shank without leaving the threads slack. Finish the threads on the wrong side in the same way as a button with holes.

BUTTONHOLES ON SHEER FABRIC

When sewing buttonholes on sheer fabric, it is important to add stability to cope with the point of stress. Silk organza is an ideal choice to give this extra support.

- Silk organza
- Transparent stabilizer
- Buttonhole foot
- Seam ripper

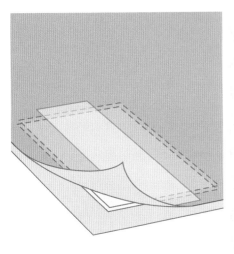

1. Place one or two layers of silk organza between the two layers of fabric and add a strip of transparent stabilizer on the surface.

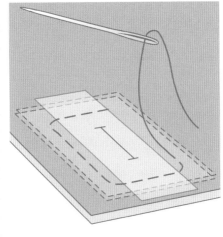

2. Tack the layers together, mark the buttonhole position on the stabilizer and select the lightweight buttonhole option.

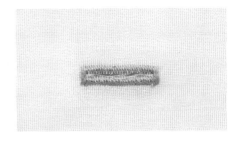

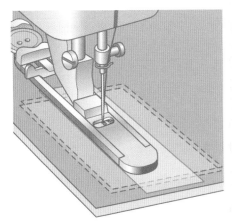

3. Sew the buttonhole into position.

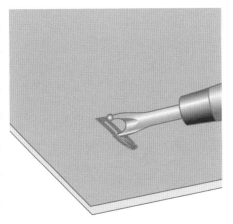

4. Secure the thread ends, then open using a seam ripper.

Sewing tips

Use a fine, new needle to sew the buttonhole.

Place a pin across the end of the buttonhole to avoid cutting too far when opening the buttonhole.

Use silk organza in the same way when sewing a button onto sheer fabric. It will help to anchor it.

Press Studs

Press studs or 'snaps' vary in size and come in plastic or in black or silver-coloured metal. They have holes that enable them to be sewn in place on a garment and are used where there is little strain. Some press studs are clamped in place with special tools and do not need to be sewn.

Hand-sewn metal press studs.

Fabric-covered press studs.

• Metal press studs

Sewing on press studs

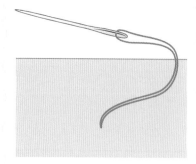

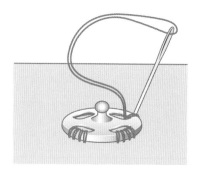

1. Mark the position of the press studs, and with a double thread, secure the end in the cloth.

2. Sew a few threads over each hole and through the fabric behind. Catch all layers beneath to secure the fastener without having the stitches showing on the wrong side.

Covering press studs

For a special, couture finish, cover press studs or snaps with fabric to make them almost invisible.

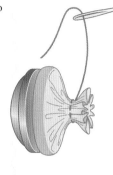

2. Sew a circle of tiny running stitches around the press stud and gather up. Finish the thread end securely and cut away all excess fabric.

1. Make a tiny snip through the centre of a small scrap of fabric and push the ball of the press stud through. Attach the other half of the press stud to hold it in place.

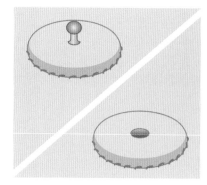

3. Repeat with the other half of the press stud, and then sew both parts in position.

HAND-BOUND BUTTONHOLE

Putting cord inside the edges of a bound buttonhole will make it more defined. These buttonholes are a suitable fastening for loose, lightweight clothing where the stress on the front band is minimal.

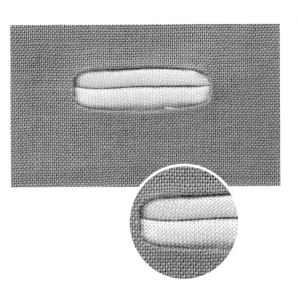

- Cord
- Fusible film

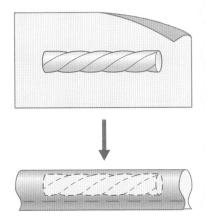

1. Cut two small strips of fabric and two pieces of cord. Wrap the fabric round the cord and tack.

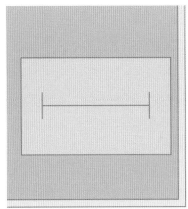

2. Cut a small piece of fusible film, draw on the outline of the buttonhole, and iron it on to the reverse of the fabric.

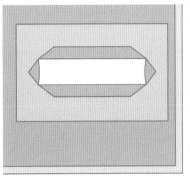

3. With the film still warm from the iron, cut into the corners and fold back the edges to reveal a letterbox shape.

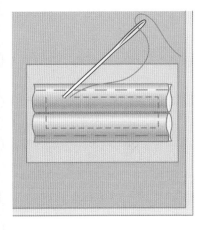

4. Arrange the cord-filled strips inside the letterbox and sew with small stitches around the edge to hold them in place.

Making a Toile

A toile is an early version of a garment made in inexpensive fabric (often calico) to test a pattern – a kind of fabric prototype. It's particularly important to make a toile when the garment you are making will be difficult or impossible to alter once it is made, for example, the Hong Kong Finish on the Outside (see page 59).

Preparation

It's important to remember that the fabric you use to make your toile must be of a similar weight and have the same drape qualities of your final fabric. If your final fabric is jersey, you will need to use a similar weight jersey for your toile.

Press your fabric and fold it in half with the grain. Place the pattern pieces on the fabric parallel to the grain line, and trace around them with a pencil. Mark on the CF (centre front) and CB (centre back), and draw in the bust lines, waist lines, the bicep line and the elbow line. Mark in the hip line and all the grain lines. It is important to mark these out so that you can see if they align with the body.

Sew your toile together with a seam allowance of 1.5cm (⅝") or the seam allowance indicated by the pattern; ensure that you are accurate throughout.

Trying on your toile

Before trying on your toile for the first time, tie some elastic around your waist – this will mark your natural waistline – and mark the fullest part of the bust and low hip on your undergarments or a leotard with sticky tape to check that these points on your body line up with the relevant points on your toile.

What is balance in a garment?

Perfect balance is when a garment's CF, CB, waist line and hip lines are aligned with the corresponding points on the body. It is important to balance your toile correctly, because all other garments will be produced from this base. Getting this right will remove the need to correct all subsequent garments that you produce using this block.

Using a dress form
If you have invested in a dress form, you could fit your toile to a dress form padded out to your own personal measurements.

Tip
To find the true CF, make a plumb line by tying a string loosely around your neck. Thread another length of string loosely through it and tie a slightly weighted object on the end. Arrange the plumb line at the CF neck and let it hang down. Mark the exact CF line with sticky tape on your undergarments or leotard, and repeat the process for the CB.

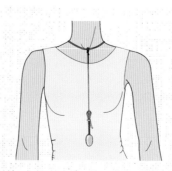

ASSESSING THE FIT OF YOUR TOILE

When you try on your toile for the first time, stand back and look at your garment in a long mirror. Assess the fit and notice the position of the balance lines on the toile. Check that the CF, CB, waist, bust and hip lines align to your own body. It is important to stand straight and look forwards. Ask someone to help you with this stage, since it can be difficult, particularly when trying to see the back. Looking down or twisting will render the assessment of fit inaccurate.

Be aware of how the garment feels on the body – the bodice should be fitted, but not tight. Notice any excess fabric or pulling across the garment. The armhole must not feel restricted, and you should be able to move your arm freely.

Remember to look at the side seams and check that they are on your sides and not drifting forwards or backwards. Taking your time to properly assess and alter the toile at this stage will be worthwhile. A perfectly fitted block will ensure that the designs you produce subsequently will fit you beautifully.

1. Check the fit

Tie a cord or length of elastic around your natural waist. Compare the tied line to the waist line marked on the toile. If, as shown here, the two lines are not the same, the waist line will need to be adjusted on the pattern.

2. Making alterations

Here, two alterations are needed. The bodice is too long and the waist is too small. To correct this, measure the difference between the elastic and the pencil line; this will give you the amount to shorten the bodice pattern by. The tightness at the waist is best adjusted by opening the side seams. Measure the amount of extra room required and add it to the pattern.

Making adjustments

Making major toile adjustments

- You will need to permanently alter your toile if any adjustments are major, and perhaps even make another. Always ensure that you make the corresponding adjustments to your pattern. Making a toile is an important part of making your own patterns, and often several are needed before the fit is completely right.

Making simple toile adjustments

- **If the toile is too big**: Pinch out any obvious excess fabric through the seams and darts of your toile, making sure that the balance lines remain straight. Mark the adjustments with a pencil, and transfer them to your pattern.
- **If the toile is too small**: Unpick the restricted area, releasing the tension. Measure the gap that is created, and add in the amounts needed where necessary.

GLOSSARY

Bias/cross grain of fabric. The diagonal direction of fabric between the warp and the weft threads.

Feed dogs Teeth that lie under the presser foot and move the fabric to allow the needle to make each stitch.

Grading When seam allowances are trimmed to different amounts to reduce bulk. Also known as layering.

Haberdashery The items required to complete a garment or project, including zips, buttons, elastic, etc.

Interfacing A stabilizing fabric used on the wrong side to support a piece of a garment, for example a collar or behind a pocket.

Interlining Also known as underlining, this is a second layer of fabric cut identically to the fashion fabric and placed against the wrong side before the garment is constructed.

Lining A separate fabric sewn on the inside of a garment to conceal all raw edges and help it to hang well.

Natural fibre Fibre from a non-synthetic source for example, cotton or flax plant, silk moth or wool.

Overlocker A machine designed to sew and finish edges in one step, although it can produce many other effects too. Also known as a serger.

Pressing cloth A fine, smooth fabric piece used to protect the surface of a fabric when ironing or pressing.

Pile Extra fibres or loops which have been woven or knitted into a fabric during manufacture, e.g., velvet or towelling.

Seam allowance The area between the sewing line and the edge of the cloth normally 1.5cm (⅝") but 2.5cm (1") in couture sewing.

Selvedge The finished edges of a cloth which do not fray.

Stabilizer(s) A material used to support fabric. Often associated with machine embroidery and normally placed under the work.

Stay stitching Stitching used to hold fabric stable and prevent it from stretching.

'Stitch in the Ditch' Used to describe where pieces are held together by stitching on the right side of a previously made seam, e.g. on a waistband.

Stretch stitch A machine stitch suitable for sewing stretch fabric – either a narrow zigzag or one which includes back stitches in its construction.

Synthetic fibre Fibres from a non-natural source. Examples are nylon, polyester and acrylic.

Tacking Temporary stitching by hand or machine. Also known as basting.

Tailor's dummy Also known as a dress form. A mannequin used to assist in the making up of garments.

Tailor's ham A small hard cushion traditionally filled with sawdust and used as a pressing aid.

Toile A test or mock-up of a garment made in a cheap cloth; also referred to as a 'muslin'.

Understitch When the seam allowances are stitched to one edge to hold it down, for example, on armhole facing.

Wadding Used in quilting, this material is a thick, soft layer of insulation sitting between the surface fabric and backing fabric. It is also known as batting.

Walking foot This replaces the standard machine foot and walks over the fabric whilst sewing avoiding the fabric 'creep' that sometimes occurs.

Zip foot An alternative machine foot. It allows the needle to get closer to the teeth of a zip than a standard machine foot.

RESOURCES

MAGAZINES

Altered Couture
www.stampington.com/html/
altered_courture.html

Butterick
www.butterick.com

McCall's
www.mccall.com

Sewing Savvy
www.clotildessewingsavvy.com

Sew Stylish
www.taunton.com

Sew News
www.sewnews.com

Sew Today
www.sewtoday.co.uk

Sewing World
www.sewingworldmagazine.
com

Threads
www.taunton.com/threads

Vogue Patterns
www.voguepatterns.com

WEBSITES

Sewing machine companies:
www.brother.com
www.elna.com
www.husqvarnaviking.com
www.janome.com
www.bernina.co.uk

www.babylock.com
www.pfaff.com
www.singer.com

Others:
www.sewingpatterns.com
Patterns from the most
popular pattern companies
on sale online.

www.isew.co.uk
Hints and tips, and news
of events.

www.sewing.org
Non-profit organization with
the aim to get people sewing.

www.besewstylish.taunton.com
Online resource and sew blogs.

www.madeiraus.com
Information about threads
and stabilizers and where
to buy them.

www.etsy.com
Global marketplace selling
materials, equipment and
finished garments.

SUPPLIERS

UK
The Berwick Street
Cloth Shop
14 Berwick Street
London W1F 0PP
020 7287 2881
www.
theberwickstreetclothshop.com

Cloth House
47 Berwick Street
London W1F 8SJ
020 7437 5155
and
98 Berwick Street
London W1F 0QJ
020 7287 1555
www.clothhouse.com

Maculloch & Wallis
25–26 Dering Street
London, W1S 1AT
020 7629 0311
www.macculloch-wallis.co.uk

Linen Me
23 Glendale Close
St Johns
Woking, GU21 3HN
www.linenme.com

USA
Reprodepot Fabrics
116 Pleasant St.
Easthampton, MA 01027
www.reprodepot.com

Sew, Mama, Sew!
PO Box 1127
Beaverton, OR 97075
(503) 380-3584
www.sewmamasew.com

Fabrics-Store.com
6325 Santa Monica Blvd.,
Ste. 102
Hollywood, CA 80038
(888) 546-3654
www.fabrics-store.com

Grayline Fabrics
260 W. 39th St.
New York, NY 10018
(212) 391-4130
www.graylinelinen.com

Create for Less
6932 S.W. Macadam Ave., Ste. A
Portland, OR 97219
(866) 333-4463
www.createforless.com

NearSea Naturals
PO Box 345
Rowe, NM 87562
(877) 573-2913
www.nearseanaturals.com

INDEX

CREDITS

Quarto would like to thank the following agencies for supplying images for inclusion in this book:

Rex Features: Pages 2, 17, 50, 83, 109, 110, 117, 119, 123, 127, 130, 133, 137, 141.
Corbis: Page 4.

All step-by-step and other images are the copyright of Quarto Publishing plc. While every effort has been made to credit contributors, Quarto would like to apologise should there have been any omissions or errors – and would be pleased to make the appropriate correction for future editions of the book.

Lorna Knight

A special thank you to Lorna Knight for additional text, supervision of photography and the creation of the following sections of the book:
Boned Cuff, pages 74–75.
Shoulder Pad, pages 76–77.
Faced Hem, pages 94–95.
Horsehair Braid Hem, pages 96–97.
Balanced Dart, pages 98–99.
Directory of Luxury Fabrics, pages 116–139.

Bogod & Company

Thank you to Bogod & Company for supplying sewing machines and equipment for photography:
Bernina Sewing Machines
Bogod & Company Ltd
91 Goswell Road
London EC1V 7EX
020 75497849
info@bernina.co.uk
www.bernina.co.uk

Thanks to the following for kindly supplying fabric for use in the book:

The Berwick Street Cloth Shop
www.theberwickstreetclothshop.com

Cloth House
www.clothhouse.com